THE MONZELLI TALES

THE MONZELLI TALES

TRUE STORIES OF A
FILM BUFF GONE WILD

JOHN GLOSKE

gatekeeper press
Where Authors are Family
Columbus, Ohio

The views and opinions expressed in this book are solely those of the author and do not reflect the views or opinions of Gatekeeper Press. Gatekeeper Press is not to be held responsible for and expressly disclaims responsibility of the content herein.

The Monzelli Tales: True Stories of a Film Buff Gone Wild

Published by Gatekeeper Press
2167 Stringtown Rd, Suite 109
Columbus, OH 43123-2989
www.GatekeeperPress.com

Copyright © 2021 by John Gloske
All rights reserved. Neither this book, nor any parts within it may be sold or reproduced in any form or by any electronic or mechanical means, including information storage and retrieval systems, without permission in writing from the author. The only exception is by a reviewer, who may quote short excerpts in a review.

Library of Congress Control Number: 2021936088

ISBN (paperback): 9781662911712
eISBN: 9781662911729

Contents

PRE-TITLE SEQUENCE	11
COPS	13
THE GENERAL	29
BLUE COLLAR	41
THE GAMBLER	53
GOING PLACES	67
SMILE	85
THE BIG HEAT	123
MEAN STREETS	141
TWO FOR THE ROAD	153
HEARTBEAT	165
NEAR DARK	179
THE LAST DETAIL	193

In Memoriam

**Dan Faris
&
Bob Shaw**

Thanks for the memories

"He was always searching for something. Afraid of anonymity. He called it the disease of our times."

Night Train (1959-Poland)

Chapter names of this book are some of the favorite films of Steve Monzelli.

PRE-TITLE SEQUENCE

(Scored by John Barry)

It was the summer of 1954 and John Wayne was the most popular movie star in the world. *The Sands of Iwo Jima, Operation Pacific, Red River*. Hit after hit cemented The Duke's status as the biggest name in Hollywood. That summer, Wayne was filming *Blood Alley* for Warner Bros. and director William "Wild Bill" Wellman at China Camp in San Pablo Bay just a few miles north of San Francisco. Living across the bay in Oakland at the same time was Tony Monzelli, a first-generation Italian-American. When Monzelli caught word that Wayne was filming nearby, he loaded up his wife, Anna, and the couple's first-born child into the family's car and drove to the location, hoping to catch a glimpse of the iconic film star. Luck struck for the Monzellis. Not only did they see Wayne, but they even had the chance to spend a few minutes talking with him. At the end of the conversation, the 47-year-old actor agreed to pose for a photo, holding 18-month-old Stephen in his arms and smiling from ear to ear. It was a simple, fleeting act of kindness on Wayne's part, but one that would have a lasting impact on the baby boy, sparking a lifelong love of cinema.

COPS

This was the start of the 1970s. Social disorder was the norm—especially in schools and most definitely in the San Francisco Bay area I called home. Student protesters filled the streets on a daily basis. If a protest wasn't happening in San Francisco, you could be certain it was happening in nearby Berkeley. Protesting the Vietnam War, advocating free love, just about any cause you could think of. School walkouts would happen at a moment's notice. Anything could happen on a school campus. Our own high school wasn't immune. One of our school administrators had just fired a popular teacher when it was discovered that the teacher was having sex with some of her male students. At least a third of the student population, mostly boys, walked out in protest. The protest didn't get the teacher rehired but the teacher was the topic of conversation around campus for some time, and a great loss to the school according to a large percentage of the male students.

A buddy of mine had his own way of causing civil disobedience. Steve Monzelli and I were standing in the hall of Rio Avenida High School, located in a small suburb about 30 miles east of San Francisco. Class was about to start and no one was in the hallway. We chatted away, most probably about some film we had just seen and then ... WHACK! Without warning, Steve had smashed the glass fire alarm on the wall next to him. I was shocked and immediately started to bolt. He grabbed my arm to stop me and calmly whispered, "John, only the guilty run. Stay here and watch what happens." The wailing alarm bell pierced the silence, then the students and teachers dutifully filed out of the classrooms, out the exit doors, and onto the lawns until the all-clear sirens were sounded. We had joined our fellow students, standing quietly, when it dawned on me: something was up. There had been false fire alarms sounded just about every day that week. The principal made a stern announcement over the public address system. He was looking for the culprit and said that when the person was caught, they would be turned over to the police department for severe punishment. Steve stood next to me, doing a great impression of an innocent high school student.

The false alarms continued. It was all part of Steve's master plan. A few days later, from a phone booth in front of a 7-Eleven across the street from campus, Steve placed a call to the principal. Covering the mouthpiece with a handkerchief he said, "I want a thousand dollars in cash, or the false alarms will continue."

The principal lost his temper. "I'll put you in jail! I'll put your parents in jail!" he screamed.

Steve calmly restated his request and told the principal he would call back in a few days with instructions on how to deliver the money, then he hung up the phone. I was totally amazed at how calm the guy could be. I'd never met someone like Steve before.

So the following day Steve smashed another fire alarm, only this time all hell broke loose as cops swarmed the campus. They stopped students and searched their belongings; they wrote down names and phone numbers. During this era, cops were not well-liked, to begin with. They were routinely referred to as 'pigs,' and this action didn't improve their standing with the students. They searched around the campus, looking into classrooms. They were literally everywhere. As far as I knew, I was the only one who knew the identity of the culprit, and I certainly wasn't talking. With such a huge show of force, Steve had to admit defeat. And he had been really looking forward to the ransom payment. Just to prove he could get away with it, he did smash an alarm a few days later, but that would be the last one, a final "fuck you" to school and the police.

Demanding ransom from a school principal was certainly the most blatant act of antisocial behavior I'd seen from Steve, but it wasn't the first. Not by a long shot. I had first met Steve years earlier while I was in the sixth grade. His brother Charlie was in my class. Steve was two years older, and one of my earliest memories of Steve was him bursting through Charlie's bedroom door one day when I was visiting after school. He nearly ripped the door off its hinges. Steve was carrying some back issues of *Famous Monsters of Filmland*. In a demanding, gruff, older-brother sort of way, he wanted to know how many issues I wanted to buy from him. I had to purchase the magazines, or he wouldn't leave the room. I gave him what little money I had to keep him quiet and so that he would leave us alone. Unfortunately, once I gave in this went on for months, and my collection of movie monster magazines grew exponentially. Almost out of necessity I began to read some of the articles; what else was I going to do with all of these magazines? Eventually, I would read anything about *The Wolfman* or various other werewolf movies. Werewolves began to intrigue me, so much so that I ordered a poster of *The Wolfman* that I could proudly hang on my bedroom wall.

On another occasion when I was visiting Charlie, Steve entered the apartment carrying a couple of cases of Coca-Cola. He handed us a couple of cans while some of his friends entered the apartment with even more cases. Steve proudly told us that this was a monthly occurrence. Apparently, a Coca-Cola delivery truck stopped next door to deliver cases to the 7-Eleven; and while the driver was inside the market, Steve and his friends looted cases from the truck.

Steve could be useful in other ways, too. Charlie called me one Saturday morning. His voice was filled with excitement. His parents had taken his brother and him to see a new movie called *Barbarella*. Charlie went on at great lengths about the various highlights of the film, but he kept coming back to the main title sequence that featured a space striptease by the star of the movie, Jane Fonda. My 14-year-old mind went wild. I immediately agreed to meet Charlie and his brother at the movie theater so I could see this tempting film. I knew I had to see it with them, because my parents rarely took me to the movies, and never to anything as wild as this.

The three of us stood in the long line for the box office. When it came time for me to buy my ticket, the cashier refused to sell me one. She sternly informed me that I had to be at least 16 or have a note from my parents. Well, I knew the note was out of the question, but Steve had a plan. We walked across the parking lot to the nearby shopping mall. Inside the mall, Steve persuaded a teenage girl to write me a note for admittance to the theater. I was shaking with nerves while back in line for the box office. *This can't work*, I thought. *I'll get in serious trouble*. The cashier read the note, looked at me, and quickly asked for my money for the ticket. *Steve is a genius*, I thought. The film was everything that Charlie and Steve said, and more. We sat through it twice.

Before long, going to the movies after school had become a ritual. Because tickets were 75 cents, we devised a way to get out of paying full price. Steve would buy one ticket, enter the cinema, simply open the side door and let Charlie and me inside. We'd then split the one ticket, 25 cents each. This worked for weeks until someone on the staff saw the light from the outside pouring into the darkened theater. We were promptly kicked out, but we sure saw a lot of films that 14-year-olds would normally not see. I recall *Targets, Rosemary's Baby*, and *The Conqueror Worm* being among my favorites.

Steve even had a plan to get us into a drive-in theater. Alan Funt, of *Candid Camera* fame, had just released his first feature, *What Do You Say To A Naked Lady*. The film was rated X, for obvious reasons. Even a fake note from a parent wouldn't get us into this must-see movie. Since Steve was now 17 he could buy a ticket. The plan was to remove the back seat from his car and have me lie down where the back seat should normally be, and hold a length of plywood over me. Charlie and Steve would then drape an old blanket over me and the plywood so that it would resemble a seat cover. Charlie was short, only about 5-foot-3, so he hunkered down under the dashboard on the passenger side and Steve threw a coat over him. It worked like a charm. The only problem I had was that there was no seat for me to sit in. I had to kneel on the plywood throughout the film, but it was certainly worth it to see so many naked ladies. It also gave us a lot to talk about at school. We had to be the only students there who had seen *What Do You Say To A Naked Lady*. The other kids in our class were very impressed with us, and I was becoming increasingly impressed with Steve's resourcefulness.

Steve didn't necessarily hate school, but he hated physical education, especially swimming, which was a little strange considering he was an excellent swimmer. But being forced into any of these activities was anathema to him. He came up with yet another plan, this one to keep him out of swimming. He bought himself a sling, medical gauze, and a box of dry plaster, and with the help of his brother was able to mix the substance and fashion a somewhat professional looking cast that covered his left arm. The teacher bought the ruse. He got to sit and watch while everyone else took to the pool. Fellow students wanted to sign the cast, but of course, he couldn't allow it; the daily re-plastering would have removed the signatures. Every day after school he would cut it off and then put it on the next morning, patching it up with fresh plaster he would mix in his parents' garage. The whole process took longer than the 50-minute P.E. class, but that didn't matter to Steve. When he put his mind to something, it didn't matter who or what stood in his way. Once, during a weekend trip to a local department store, Steve and I ran into one of his teachers. The teacher was glad to see that Steve had finally had his cast removed. "It's only off for the weekend," Steve explained. "The doctor wants my arm to breathe." Sure enough, come Monday morning, the cast was back.

You could always count on Steve to ask an inappropriate question. He would phrase the query in such a manner that you never knew if he was kidding, serious, or just plain stupid. Once during a discussion on the reproductive system during sex education class, Steve's hand shot up: "But *how* do you get the girl to let you fertilize her egg?" It was a true Monzelli moment. The teacher blushed, big time. He had no answer other than to tell Steve to shut up.

Steve's life revolved around movies, and by this time his obsession for films had started to rub off on me. Sure, I liked movies—what kid didn't? Steve knew movies inside and out. He knew the actors' names, their credits and biographies, and plots of movies I had never heard of. This guy was amazing. By my early high school years, movies were front and center in our lives. We would argue films with all the fervor of a college debate club arguing the pros and cons of the Vietnam War. Feverish arguments would include such important topics as: was it Stan 'Laurel' or 'Lawrel' (as Oliver Hardy pronounced it)? Was *The Bank Dick* the best W.C. Fields film or was it *It's a Gift*? Were black-and-white films inherently better than color films? And of course, the unending film buff argument: who was the better Dracula? Bela Lugosi or Christopher Lee? These were only a few of the perplexing questions that we would argue endlessly.

Just because a film might be 40 or 50 years old was of no concern to us. The release date was unimportant. Was it an interesting film? That was our only concern. Silent-film great Buster Keaton was a particular favorite of Steve's. Keaton's films played constantly in revival theaters around the Bay Area while we were in high school. Steve's nickname for me at the time was Keaton because he insisted that like the silent comic, I never smiled. Armed with a Super 8mm camera, Steve started to make his own films. He remade gags from some of Keaton's films, along with Laurel and Hardy, to fit into his own movies. The films were pretty impressive. Especially the one where he grabs onto a speeding San Francisco cable car from a standing position. Upon grabbing the cable car he is whisked into the air, just like Keaton. It must have hurt like hell, but it sure got a laugh when he showed it in class one day.

Steve Monzelli remakes a Buster Keaton gag for one of his own 8mm movies using a cable car in San Francisco.

He cranked out these short films endlessly, and they were not always comedies. One film was a mafia drama starring his father. He shocked the class and the teacher when in one scene, his father, playing a mafia don, is shown lying in a bathtub taking a bubble bath while shouting orders on a telephone. When he finishes the call he stands up to get out of the tub and is shown completely naked. The students' first question to Steve was how he got his father to do a nude scene.

Money to see a movie could be difficult to come by, but Steve as always had a plan to pick up some additional cash. The local mall had a rather large and deep fountain, surrounded by a wishing well people would throw coins into. Steve, wearing slip-on sandals, would walk up to the well and eye the area with the largest coin deposits. He would then slip off his sandals, pull up his pant legs, and wade into the wishing well. Quickly he would scoop up large amounts of the wet coins and fill his pockets with them. Charlie and I would stand off in the distance watching him in action. Steve would do this about every other week. Occasionally a security guard would spot him, but Steve would jump out, put his sandals back on and sprint for the exit doors. He was a great runner and up to this point had never been caught by an authority figure.

Steve was a senior in high school when he discovered Mecca … well, Mecca for film buffs anyway. It was a small retail shop in a rundown area of San Francisco called Hunters Point. The store: Cinema Treasures. It was originally called Attic Treasures and they specialized in antiques of all kinds, but soon its proprietor Patrick discovered that "hippies love old movie posters," hence the name change. Patrick and his wife were fairly new to the city. As Patrick was fond of saying, "We wanted to be hippies too, but we didn't have enough money." It was great to find others who shared our love for old movies. What little extra cash we had as teens was spent at the store buying stills, posters, and lobby cards. Patrick knew what we collected and would put any items aside he thought we might like. Cinema Treasures would be our hangout for years to come.

The Steve McQueen movie *Bullitt* had been released a few years earlier but still held a grip on Steve, and now that he owned his first car he could actually live the movie. He had an 8-track player installed in his car and promptly purchased the soundtrack, composed by Lalo Schifrin. Steve knew the exact filming locations for the famous chase that took place on the hills of San Francisco. It was well past midnight when Steve and I, along with a friend from school, climbed into his car. When we arrived at the actual location of the chase, Steve slammed in the tape, cranked up the volume, hit the gas pedal, and took off in a flash. With acknowledgment to the original movie stunt team, I think Steve did a better job. It sure was more thrilling, doing it live and in the dead of night. His car flew over the steep hills of San Francisco. When it came back down to earth it would bottom out and leave a long trail of sparks flying into the darkness. This would cause Steve to let out a scream of joy. Steve had such a good time that these reenactments became a regular occurrence. A call from Steve saying, "Do you want to play *Bullitt*," was all that was needed for a late night of entertainment. It also made for great conversation at school the following day. Steve was quickly getting a reputation as something of a wild man.

The streets of San Francisco were not the only areas where Steve plied his stunt driving skills. He also developed an affinity for driving over lawns around our neighborhood. The more continuous lawns the better; as long as trees and bushes didn't get in the way, he could run over two or three lawns in a row. He delighted in pointing out the lawns he crossed the following day.

It is not uncommon to read influential books while in high school. *To Kill A Mockingbird*, *Atlas Shrugged* and the like continue to be read and enjoyed and influence many young readers. In high school, Steve found such a book, a book I doubt anyone else in school was reading—*My Wicked Wicked Ways*, Errol Flynn's autobiography.

This posthumously published memoir became Steve's blueprint for his life's journey. He even found lessons in the book that I had never found when I read it. Years later, he told me that he learned about putting cocaine on the tip of his penis before having sex from the book; he said it made him last longer. His growing love of vodka was also based on Flynn's love of the same drink.

Steve eventually graduated from high school. Not exactly on time; he had to return the following year, after his class graduated, to make up a couple of classes. As I was two years behind him, it gave me a chance to have him in one of my classes. Formal education was never a priority for Steve—the priorities were movies, girls, and drinking, in changing order of importance.

As ardent film buffs, we were also collectors. Movie posters, soundtracks, almost any film-related material, we wanted it. We discovered a business named National Screen Service. They were a distribution network supplying advertising materials to movie theaters. NSS was located in an industrial area in San Francisco. Their rear entrance was located in a quiet alley, and the back door was sometimes left open. If it was, we would sneak up the wooden staircase, open the door to the trash area, and take whatever goodies happened to be in the garbage cans. You had to be as silent as a mouse because the door to their office was opposite the trash area. We would usually check out the trash cans once a week. It was an outing, something for us to look forward to. We eventually learned the trash pickup date, which ensured we'd never miss a full garbage can. They would toss out hordes of movie stills, posters, press-books, and 35mm trailers, which we would later splice onto reels and show during off-hours at the movie theater I worked at.

One day we hit the jackpot. The garbage cans were stuffed full and in short order, my car was now stuffed full, the trunk and backseat filled with movie items. We made trip after trip, up and down the stairs, filling the car. We couldn't believe our good fortune. We had never had a haul like this. We climbed in the car to make our getaway when three employees of NSS came bursting out of the alley doorway, screaming at us to stop. I would have just taken off, but one guy was standing in front of the car, waving his hands furiously and screaming like a banshee, "We have your license plate number! We called the police!" They had us. There was no escape. We felt like Cagney, Raft, or Bogart in a Warner Bros. gangster epic. They yelled that we'd be arrested if we did not put all the garbage back. It was a sad task, but we did what we were told, and they let us go with a very stern warning to never return. Patrick came up with an idea of paying off the garbageman so that he would deliver the garbage to us before going to the city dump, but the idea sounded too far-fetched and didn't go any further. We would still drive by on occasion, and even sneak up the staircase, but the garbage room door was now always locked. Our source for free movie memorabilia had dried up, but it was great while it lasted.

Steve always seemed to have novel ways to make cash. While most of us in high school worked at fast-food restaurants or, in my case, a movie theater, Steve was much more creative. I don't think that having a regular legitimate job ever entered into his conscious mind. It was always the sneaky ways that appealed to him. One quick way to get some money was to steal cans of beer from his old man. Over the course of a few weeks, Steve could collect a couple of dozen cans of beer without his father ever noticing. On the night of a big school dance, or some other activity on the campus, Steve would wait outside the event and sell the beers to students eager for a drink. It was always a big moneymaker for him. A longer-range plan was to collect comic books. Anytime a new comic book character was introduced, Steve would purchase three or four issues, wrap them in plastic, and store them away for future selling. He seemed to have some foresight into what would one day be valuable. To me they were comic books, you read them and then give them away, but to Steve, they were an investment.

Somehow, Steve acquired a .22 caliber starter pistol, the type used at sporting events to signal the start of a foot race. They shoot only blanks, but the gun looked real and certainly sounded realistic. He loved carrying the pistol and he loved the mischief it could create. Once while we were watching a movie along with his brother in the crowded Hayward Theater, Steve waited for a quiet moment in the film, then sprung from his seat and yelled, "Die, you bastards!" and began firing the pistol indiscriminately. The flash from the pistol's muzzle created a frightening look in the darkened theater. Screams from the audience added to the surreal effect. Fortunately, we were sitting next to an exit. We sprang from our seats and bolted out the door, sprinting through the parking lot and into the safety of the street. I was pissed. I wanted to see the end of the film and I happened to like the theater. I figured it would be months before I could get up the nerve to go back there again. Steve just laughed the whole thing off.

The pistol caused some other problems. One day, the three of us went to a local donut shop. Outside the shop was a newspaper vending machine. I put in my quarter for a paper. We needed to check the movie listings. At the exact time the quarter dropped in the slot, Steve fired his starter's pistol at the machine. I grabbed the paper and unbeknownst to us, it looked to the employees like Steve had shot the lock off the newspaper dispenser. We then entered the store. The woman behind the counter seemed awfully nervous, but it didn't dawn on me as to why. As we checked out the movie listings, trying to decide which film to see that day, the place began to clear out. Within minutes, two cop cars arrived and officers jumped out, guns drawn. They grabbed Steve and threw him against the wall and patted him down. Steve smiled and treated it as a joke, but the cops weren't laughing. They told him how serious the matter was. One cop yelled at him, "It's the wrong era to be carrying a gun around." His brother and I sat motionless. The cops took Steve outside for questioning. After a few minutes, they decided to call Steve's father and let him deal with his son. They let Charlie and me go but took Steve back to his house. The cops told Steve and his father that although this type of pistol was legal, he should only use it at a track meet. I swear that Steve's father wished that they would have just kept Steve.

Next to the donut shop was a pizza parlor. They made a pretty good pizza. They made it the old-fashioned way by tossing the dough high in the air and spinning it around above their heads. Good stuff. But Steve liked to cause trouble. Using a payphone he called up the owner, Gino, and told him off. "Gino, I ate your pizza last night and it was shit. I've never tasted such a horrible pizza!" The owner exploded, swearing into the phone. Steve countered with, "Shut the fuck up, you bastard. If you yell at me, I'll come down to your restaurant and beat the shit out of you." That only made Gino so enraged that he wanted to fight. Steve made a date. "I'm going to be down there in one hour, you asshole. Be prepared. I'm going to beat the shit out of you for making such lousy pizzas." Steve hung up the phone and turned to me and said, "Let's go to the restaurant."

I was shocked. "Steve, he'll kill us!" I told him.

Steve calmly replied, "He doesn't know who we are. Let's just order a pizza and watch him."

As we sat waiting for him to cook our pizza, Gino paced back and forth. He looked like a shark, waiting to go in for the kill. Visibly upset. When the time came for the appointment he was even more on edge. Gino marched back and forth from the counter to the front door, looking for the disgruntled patron and waiting to strike out in vengeance. We just ate our pizza casually and then left. Steve stopped at the phone booth again and placed another call to Gino. Steve yelled into the mouthpiece, "Gino, you bastard, I was busy tonight so I couldn't come in. But I'll be there tomorrow to beat the shit out of you!"

With that, he hung up the phone. "That will give him something to think about," Steve said to me, grinning and walking out of the booth.

When I graduated from high school, my parents due to some lapse of reasoning let me take the long drive down to southern California to spend a couple of days at Disneyland with Steve and Charlie. The Sergio Leone film *Duck You Sucker* had been released at about the same time. The film did little box office, even after a change of title. But the film did leave an impression on Steve. The evening at Disneyland began with us taking the Peter Pan ride, go figure! We were riding in the hanging baskets high over darkened London when Steve got up, got out, and hung by his fingertips over the side of the basket. He was just tall enough to kick over the tops of Big Ben and other famous monuments. We helped him get back inside just before the basket was to exit through the huge doors and back outside to the park.

One basket ride wasn't enough. We decided to jump in the Skyway baskets that take you from one side of the park to the other. Once up, far from the crowd below, Steve pulled out some firecrackers. He struck a match, touched it to the fuse and tossed the package into the crowd below, yelling out, "Duck, you sucker!" The firecrackers exploded about halfway down. The patrons must have thought it was just part of the Disneyland fireworks show. When we exited the basket we were immediately met by a security detail and ushered off to a section of Disneyland most tourists never see. Steve admitted that he was indeed responsible for the firecrackers, and that Charlie and I did not know he was going to do it, which was true. After an hour or so of questioning, they ordered Steve off the property, and he was instructed that he was not to return for a month. Charlie and I could return to the park if we wished; but as Steve had the car, we had to leave with him.

THE GENERAL

Nobody referred to Steve's father by his proper name. Everyone just called him "The Old Man." And it wasn't always a term of endearment.

The Old Man was technically a father, but only in the strictest sense of the word. Wisdom, guidance, and compassion just weren't in his DNA. If they were, I rarely saw it. Neither did his two sons, or anyone else for that matter. The Old Man loved listening to jazz, watching TV, drinking any available alcohol, and smoking dope (often doing all four simultaneously). He loved to hang around Steve and our group of friends like some kind of older brother. No matter what we were up to, he seemed to always be around. He didn't want to miss anything. The Old Man was the loudest person in our group, always talking but saying little. He was unlike any father I'd ever seen. He looked the part of a 1950s beatnik with his shiny, slicked-back hair, mustache, and goatee.

Eventually The Old Man wanted Steve out of the house. As Steve was now in his early twenties, it wasn't an unreasonable request. Steve rarely paid rent (he didn't have the money even if he wanted to), so demanding payment was a lost cause. That didn't stop The Old Man from trying. They had been fighting for weeks when one afternoon Steve asked me if I would accompany him to his house. The two had gotten into a bad fight the night before, that had only ended when Steve's mom stepped in to break it up. I had never heard her lose her temper or even raise her voice, but apparently, she did that time, and it worked to calm the situation.

When I pulled up to the curb The Old Man was already sweating like a pig, as he piled Steve's possessions on the front lawn. From the look of it, the job was nearly complete. Only The Old Man looked as if he was about ready to have a heart attack.

"He's at it again, John. Help me get my stuff back in the house," Steve requested matter-of-factly.

"Steve, he wants *you* out!" I fired back.

"He pulls this shit all the time, it's no big deal," Steve replied.

As with most of Steve's explanations, I accepted it. As I helped Steve haul his belongings back inside, The Old Man screamed, "John, I want him out of here! What can I do?"

I didn't have an answer for The Old Man. His response was to go inside, crack a can of beer, and sit on the couch while we restocked Steve's bedroom. It was an uncomfortable situation, to say the least.

When Steve and his father were not fighting, The Old Man would follow us from bar to bar in San Francisco, looking to get laid. It puzzled me at the time since he had a devoted wife at home, and we were so much younger than he was; but he loved being with us. He was as eager as a 20-year-old in a whorehouse. He loved talking to young girls, giving them lines of bullshit about his many "accomplishments," shaving 10 or 20 years off his actual age (he was approaching 50 years old at the time).

The tone of the relationship between Steve and his father went from simmer to boil constantly. There was never a time that it felt like a normal father-and-son relationship. When it hit boiling point, all hell could break loose, and it frequently did. When Steve finally moved out, it was into a small studio apartment in the Lake Merritt area of Oakland. The Old Man knew the building's owner so Steve received a break in the rent, but it did little to improve their contentious relationship. One night, The Old Man was over for a visit. For some reason—and there didn't have to be a reason—a fight broke out between them and it got ugly quick. Steve had The Old Man on the ground and was beating the shit out of him. The building was old, with thick lath and plaster walls, but noise from the family fisticuffs echoed up and down the hallway. Someone called the cops and they were on the scene in a flash. Upon arriving, they found The Old Man in the hallway a bruised and bloody mess. Steve barricaded himself inside his apartment and refused to come out. Ever the film buff, he transformed himself into Cody Jarrett from *White Heat*. James Cagney played Jarrett expertly in the classic film, but Steve gave him a run for his money. "Come and get me, coppers!" he shouted. "No one takes Cody Jarrett alive!"

With the cops seconds from breaking down the door, Steve shouted, "I made it, Ma! Top of the world!" And with that, a stampede of armed officers busted inside the small studio. They tackled Steve, put him in a straightjacket, strapped him onto a gurney, and hauled him away to a waiting ambulance. Stunned neighbors peered outside their front doors to watch the entire spectacle unfold in the hallway. As he passed one young boy, Steve let out a howl that would have made The Wolfman proud, frightening the youngster and causing him to flee into the arms of his father. Steve spent the next two days in a mental hospital, playing basketball mostly, but also in discussion with a doctor about his anger management issues.

The Old Man's frustration with his son was sometimes justified. Sitting around a table in a bar one night with some of Steve's friends, The Old Man, who was a World War II veteran, was telling tales of his time in the European theater. The drinks had been flowing for some time when Steve spoke up, slurring his words: "Did you ever kill any Krauts?"

"No, but I shot at a bunch of *Italians*!" The Old Man shot back loudly.

"Why were you doing that?" Steve asked indignantly.

"Because they were shooting at me!" The Old Man answered.

Apparently, Steve had no clue about Italy's role in the war. His father was dejected. "I give up," he said. "All the time I spent fighting in the war was totally wasted if my own son has no idea why I was shooting at Italians."

The Old Man had an uncle. In his younger days, the uncle had been a prizefighter of some renown, but those glory days had long since passed and dementia had set in, most likely due to all the blows to his head he had endured. The uncle loved to talk to anyone who would listen. He would even talk to those around who refused to listen, but he mostly spoke Italian. He was nice enough, but you had to stand clear when the phone rang because he would immediately start to swing his fists as if he were fighting Joe Louis. One night the three of them—The Old Man, his uncle, and Steve—decided to go out drinking. The uncle was supposed to be the designated driver; so much for that. Late into the evening, the uncle excused himself to use the restroom but instead took off in the car without telling Steve and The Old Man. Stranded in some dive bar in Oakland, the two were forced to take a taxi home (you can imagine how that went). The uncle didn't show up until dinner the following day and he had some bad news: The Old Man's prized Cadillac DeVille was a wreck. From trunk to hood, the entire passenger side of the once sleek-looking car was smashed in; the scrapes came in all colors of the rainbow, indisputable evidence that the driver had hit a myriad of cars. His memory shot from all the drinking, the uncle had no explanation for what happened (or how he had arrived home). It wasn't long after this incident that The Old Man found other living arrangements for his uncle.

The Old Man liked it loud. I mean everything. He would play jazz music throughout the house and still have the television turned all the way up. The jazz music was mesmerizing. This wasn't the music of my generation, but for some reason, I connected with it and it connected with me. Fleetwood Mac, The Who; they were the big bands of that day. I would listen to popular rock music but to me, jazz had a much more complex feel. The Old Man loved to share stories of 1940s Oakland when jazz was the most popular music of the day. Jazz clubs lined downtown. People would dress in their finest clothes for a night on the town. The streets of Oakland were considered safe. He talked of the greats that he saw play live—Miles Davis, Stan Getz, and the like. Those were his glory days, and he relived them by constantly playing his massive record collection. It was infectious, at least for me. After listening to his music I couldn't enjoy listening to rock like I used to. When I would enter his house, The Old Man would shout, "It's John Glory-ow-sky!" Not the correct pronunciation of my name, of course, and he knew it. But I liked it. I was always "Glory-ow-sky" to The Old Man, and he always yelled it out for all to hear. He would then crank up the record player even louder and go back to laying on the couch. He must have known his love for jazz was rubbing off.

I was still in high school when I realized The Old Man was not like any of the other fathers I knew. At 17, I had driven over to pick up Steve and his brother one night so the three of us could go to San Francisco to see *Anthony Adverse*, a classic film at a revival theater named the Gateway Cinema, within walking distance of Fisherman's Wharf. Upon arriving at their house, The Old Man asked me if I wanted a fresh-baked brownie, right out of the oven.

"Sure, I'll take a couple to go," I said naively.

Steve and his brother refused the offer. On the way to the city, I munched on the brownies while driving across the Bay Bridge. *Yeah, The Old Man may be a pain in the ass, but he can bake a mean brownie,* I thought to myself.

During the early part of the Mervyn LeRoy drama, I began to feel light-headed. Then the theater began to sway. I told Steve I felt weird.

"It's nothing," he whispered. "It's just all the brownies you ate. My dad always puts too much grass in them. That's why I don't like them. He always overdoes it."

So I spent the next two hours melting into my seat, half-coherent, mind elsewhere. I remember that I really wanted to see the film. After the credits rolled I was so fucked up that I couldn't even tell you what the movie was about. I could have been watching *Lassie Come Home* for all I know. I do remember that it seemed very long.

The Old Man's histrionics did come in handy once. I went to a job interview in Oakland and the owner of a process-serving business hired me on the spot. He even asked me if I knew anyone else looking for a job. I of course mentioned Steve and the owner told me to bring him in later that day, which I did, and Steve was also hired without delay. The job paid well and we could make our own hours, which was great; being young and devoted film buffs, we didn't want to be tied down to a full-time job. There would be plenty of time for 9-to-5 jobs later on, we thought. Later in the day, we told The Old Man about our good fortune.

"Are you fucking crazy?" he yelled to our surprise. "You two are going to be process servers in Oakland! You're gonna get shot dead on your first day!"

After a few more minutes of being yelled at, Steve and I both decided The Old Man had a point and changed our minds about the job. We never bothered to show up for work, and the owner never called us to see where his new process servers were. I figured he probably knew we had come to our senses.

The Old Man had been on disability for years. He had been a carpenter and at one point was injured on a construction site. The injury never seemed to slow him down, but he was officially "disabled," which gave him more free time to hang around us. He was always open for job opportunities, but only if they paid in cash. One day he answered a newspaper ad for actors needed for a movie to be shot in San Francisco. The ad was placed by the Mitchell Brothers, who were best known for their classy porno films like *Behind the Green Door* and *Resurrection of Eve*. They were responsible for starting the 'porno chic' movement of the early '70s. Well, The Old Man called the phone number on the ad, and the fellow who answered the phone hired him immediately. The amazing thing was The Old Man was probably the only adult male in the Bay Area who didn't know who the Mitchell Brothers were. Besides their movies, they owned a popular San Francisco strip club that featured a huge undersea mural on an exterior wall that faced a very busy street. If you looked closely at the underwater plants, you could see that some of the vegetation resembled vaginas. We always delighted in seeing the mural and passed it often on our visits to Cinema Treasures.

When The Old Man arrived on the set, he finally realized just what type of film was being made. He refused to undress, so he took a job as an extra. His scene involved a party in which he is seen standing behind a large champagne glass that contained a naked woman holding a ladle, who was constantly pouring champagne over various parts of her body. The Old Man had finally made it in the movies. His son was not the only one who harbored that dream. At the end of the shoot, he was paid $50 for one day's work. The money came in handy because when he returned to his car, someone had stolen his battery. The new battery cost him $50. The movie was released on VHS at the dawn of the home video era. In just a few years we would get the honor of owning copies of The Old Man's big-screen debut.

The day with the Mitchell Bros. would not be The Old Man's only foray into the exploding world of the porn business circa the late '70s. The Old Man had a buddy who worked as a projectionist at a downtown Oakland movie theater. Dangelo was his name and he was a fellow Italian, but due to his size and girth, he looked more like a balding grizzly bear. Dangelo owned a small storefront near downtown Oakland that he used as a storage area for his collection of 35mm films and various projector parts, along with being his private screening room. Dangelo had designs on becoming a movie producer, and with the help of The Old Man, they hatched a plan. Dangelo would use his movie camera that he had obtained long ago in his Army days during World War II to shoot people having sex. Their plan was to make a cheap porno film, then turn around and use the profits to make some sort of legitimate film they could be proud of (and make tons of money with, of course).

The budding filmmaking duo bought an advertisement in the popular underground newspaper *The Berkeley Barb*, asking for young women to audition. The ad requested the wannabe starlets to arrive at the storefront on a Saturday morning. Dangelo and The Old Man arrived that Saturday a couple of hours early. They figured if they were lucky they might have three or four women show up. They were shocked to find almost a dozen lined up when they arrived.

Once they were ready to shoot the auditions, they picked out a half-dozen or so of the "cute ones" and prepared the studio for the shoot. The "studio" really wasn't much, nor was the set. They simply spread a drop cloth on the cement floor and then covered that with a couple of old Army blankets. One by one they had the wannabe actresses face the camera, smile, then remove their clothing and then smile a little more. When they completed the auditions they realized they had a reel or two of film left, so they asked for volunteers to shoot the rehearsal for the orgy scene. By this time, even more "actresses" had arrived so that now they had ten or so women, all strangers to each other. They all willingly stripped, and then kissed, fondled, and went down on each other in a flesh frenzy worth of *Jaws*. All the while Dangelo filmed away, shouting directions. Meanwhile, The Old Man stood nearby, "supervising."

When The Old Man bragged about his new movie production, I really had my doubts that it existed. I'd heard too much of his bullshit just to blindly believe anything he said. However, one night a few months after the shoot, Dangelo invited Steve and me over to the studio to watch his personal 35mm print of *You Only Live Twice*. We drank beer and enjoyed watching one of our favorite James Bond films. When the film ended, Dangelo, who was very drunk by this time, told us he had a surprise. He put on the porno reels he had shot with The Old Man. I couldn't believe they had found so many willing women to do such things … and most amazing of all, they didn't have to pay them! The feature they had planned was never made, but they did say that some of the women who auditioned called frequently to see if they had been chosen for roles. Their answer was always the same: "We're still looking at the auditions."

Not long after the screening, Steve called in a panic early one morning. "Meet me at Carter's Donuts in Oakland as soon as you can," he said in a serious tone. "Oh, and bring a rope so we can tow a car."

I had known Steve for long enough to know that I shouldn't ask any questions, just do as I was told. And I did. When I met up with him he looked worried and nervous, not normal emotions for my friend. It turned out that Steve had borrowed The Old Man's Cadillac the night before. The Old Man had had the car completely restored to its former glory since his uncle had taken it for a joy ride.

The previous night, Steve had met a girl in a bar, and after they had both consumed enough alcohol he persuaded her to leave the bar to find a secluded area for sex. Steve took her up in the hills above the MacArthur Freeway. It was pitch black, sometime after midnight, and he was guiding the behemoth of a car along a dirt hiking path. Suddenly Steve made a wrong turn and drove halfway off a cliff. The car got stuck; it wouldn't move an inch. Since he couldn't move the car any farther, he decided it was as good a place as any for sex with his new bar friend. Unfortunately for Steve, the girl had lost interest, and now she was pissed and wanted to go home. After she yelled at him for a few minutes for getting her in this predicament, she got out of the car and started to hike down the hill in the darkness, never to be seen by Steve again. But what to do about the car? Steve's idea was to tie a rope to the bumper of my car and use it to pull his father's car back onto the dirt road.

I drove up to the scene and told Steve, "There is no way in hell I can pull your car." As I went into a further explanation for him, we noticed another car approaching. It was Oakland PD. We both looked at each other in amazement. How did they find this place?" I asked Steve. He shook his head.

When they got closer, I noticed The Old Man in the back seat of the cop car. It turned out that The Old Man had been contacted by the police, who had found the car earlier in the morning and assumed it was stolen. The Old Man was ranting and raving at Steve while the cops were on their radio calling for a tow truck. With The Old Man ramping up his volume, Steve turned to me and said with a Steve McQueen smile, "All I wanted to do was get laid."

It would not be the last time that trying to get laid would lead to serious problems.

BLUE COLLAR

The mid-1970s would be the final few years before the advent of home video. We had no inkling that the whole world of film buffs was about to change. These were the days when if you wanted to see some obscure 1930s John Ford film, you either waited for a possible one-time, late-night showing on TV, or hoped beyond hope that it was booked into some repertory cinema in the big city.

Fortunately for us, the Bay Area was overflowing with these venues. Market Street in San Francisco in particular was loaded with grand old movie palaces. They were all past their prime, but places like The Pix, The Powell, and St. Francis often showed triple bills of all types of interesting films. Some of the theaters still showed serials, which I found astounding since they were at least two decades old by that point.

Some of the theaters were little more than dark, dank flea pits. The Berkeley Repertory Cinema stands out in that regard. But what these venues lacked in cleanliness they more than made up for in quality programming: Marx Brothers triple features, W.C. Fields festivals. The threat of disease or stabbing weren't enough to keep us from going. One night at the Berkeley "Rep," as it was known, we sat through a double feature while the guy behind me placed his bare feet on my seat's armrest. Since it was raining outside I wondered what had happened to his shoes, but since this was Berkeley you didn't ask those questions. Also, this being Berkeley, a lot of the audience seemed bathed in patchouli oil. It was a favorite fragrance among the hippie clientele. On the rare occasion I smell the fragrance today, it brings me right back to all the nights we spent at that theater.

Unlike at modern-day cinemas, the restroom at the Berkeley Rep was just to the right of the big screen. If you had to relieve yourself during a film, it meant walking in front of the entire audience, opening the door, turning on a light, and then entering the room the size of a small closet. Once the light was turned on the audience inevitably yelled, "Shut the door!" You had to be quick. It was another flea pit of a theater, but they certainly knew how to program. We would scan the newspaper every Wednesday to make sure we never missed an important movie. If it meant traveling across the Bay, or to some dangerous neighborhood, no matter, we went.

Once a year there was the San Francisco International Film Festival. Their lineup of in-person tributes was fantastic. The setup made for a long day, but if you were a film buff it was the only place to be during the two-week run. They would show a film associated with the guest at 10 a.m. followed by an in-person tribute that consisted of film clips and a question-and-answer session, and then another feature to wrap up. It was movie-lover heaven. We would often spend eight hours or more immersed in film history. We saw such cinema icons as Frank Capra, Raoul Walsh, Jack Nicholson, Lillian Gish, James Wong Howe, Ruth Gordon, Akira Kurosawa, Jack Lemmon, and Sam Peckinpah ("If you don't like my movies you can kiss my ass!"). We cheered upon hearing this. As did almost half the audience. During Capra's tribute, I asked the first question: "Do you plan on making any more films?" The audience cheered, but he responded with a quick "NO."

One of the most memorable tributes was to Rita Hayworth. She had requested they show *Road to Salina*, a gutsy move on her part as it was a film she had recently made, not one of her well-known classics. After the screening, during the Q&A segment, a guy wearing a long overcoat stood up and yelled for all of us to hear, "Ms. Hayworth, I'm wearing your costume from *Gilda*, I wanted you to see it!" He removed his overcoat to reveal the iconic dress. The audience roared with approval. She graciously replied, "It looks very good on you," causing the crowd to break into cheers again.

Watching movies and attending festivals was great, but one did have to earn some money to afford these things, not to mention all the movie posters we were buying. Fortunately, Steve had found the way a couple of years earlier. It was the best of both worlds: a quick way to earn some cash and a great place to meet girls. The venues: Oakland Coliseum and Candlestick Park in San Francisco. Steve felt he was a king and these ballparks were his kingdom.

Steve had begun selling concessions (peanuts, popcorn, ice cream, etc.) when he was still a teenager, but when he turned 21 he hit the big time by now getting to sell beer. That meant more money in his pocket. Plus, being a beer vendor puts you on the top of the vendor food chain. Since Steve was a veteran, he eventually got me on staff. All his talk of quick money and girls was too much to resist.

It's hard to imagine that the act of selling beer in a ballpark would involve a strict hierarchy, but it did, a hierarchy the new guys were subjected to and repeatedly reminded that they had no chance of breaking into. Steve was young but already considered an old-timer. He was a union member at this point, which meant that when we showed up for work, he wouldn't talk to me and barely acknowledged my existence. This was not his doing, it was the system. It was later explained to me that the longtime union members didn't want the new kids on the block taking their jobs. So I was shunned, along with any other new guy who got a job there. At least I could talk to the new hires; that was fine with me.

There was one old-timer who really got on my nerves. His name was Jimmy and he was a tall guy with a huge head of hair. I was told he was an attorney and sold beer just to make extra money. I'm not sure that was true, but everyone understood it as fact. I thought at the time that there must be more money in being an attorney, but maybe not. Jimmy would pass me on an aisle and yell out, "Hey son, you're in my way!" or "Hey son, get out of my aisle." He had a condescending way and he always yelled just loud enough so that everyone within view could hear him. It took a while for me to remedy this situation.

One night he yelled out, "Hey son, do you have change for a 20?" I fired back, "Sure, anything for you, Dad!" After a couple of weeks of calling him "Dad" he stopped calling me "son." Actually, he stopped talking to me altogether until I had been there about a year. One night he came over and told me, "You're probably wondering why we never talk to you." Then he explained the situation, which Steve had explained long before. I didn't really care if Jimmy or any of the other old-timers talked to me, because I didn't really care to talk to them either. When I was able to join the union, I kept talking to the new non-union employees. That really pissed off the old-timers.

Steve was a big guy by then, six-foot-two and in great physical shape. Carrying cases of bottled beer up and down cement staircases at the ballpark was no great effort for him. It also had the side benefit of supplying him with free beer while he worked. He would down a cold one, and then simply smash the bottom of the bottle on a staircase, then tell the office that his case contained a broken bottle. It was that easy. Finding girls took even less effort. "John, if you want something, just go for it," he would say with a smile. He thought nothing of asking any girl out, even if she was sitting with some guy who could be her husband. "The only question I ask any woman is what time does your husband come home?" he would say. I knew the line was from the

Western drama *Hud,* but no one else seemed to know. I told Steve once, "You should pay the screenwriters for all their dialog you use."

"But John, it works," he replied with a smile. He wasn't lying.

If he couldn't pick up a woman at the ballpark, there was always Sam's Hof Brau. Located just outside the parking lot area of the Oakland Coliseum, it was the place to go after a game for a drink and a bite to eat. Steve came up with a novel way to meet women at Sam's. During baseball season, he would pass himself off as a relief pitcher for the opposing team. During winter, he would assume the identity of a hockey player for whatever opposing team happened to be in town. With his dark, Italian good looks, Steve could easily talk himself into a group of women. His approach would inevitably include lines from films he'd seen. He loved quoting the line from *The Gambler,* "All poets and athletes know that two and two equal five." I wasn't sure what the line meant, but it worked for Steve; maybe the women didn't know what it meant either, but they seemed to think it meant Steve was an intellectual.

He would thrill the group with stories of various towns he had played in, or the difficult plays he had been involved in. He was so convincing that he almost had me believing his stories. After a half-dozen beers or so, he would go off with one, or perhaps two, of the women he would meet at Sam's. He would always insist on going to their house since he was supposedly from "out of town."

I would sometimes wonder what would have happened if one of the many women Steve seduced in this manner were to find out the truth. A woman's treasured memory of a night of passionate sex with a professional sports player would be totally shattered if she found out her one-time lover was just a guy who hocked beer at the ballpark. As far as I know, none of the women ever found out the truth.

During work, Steve would always have an eye open for a cute girl. One night his good friend Eddie found two, Lisa and Debbie. He had seen them before, even flirted with them, but they would never go out with him. The girls only wanted to go out with the players, and it was too late for Steve and Eddie to pass themselves off as pros when they had a case of beer hanging off their shoulders. Eddie alerted Steve about them. Steve spent most of the game flirting with them, and by the end of the game, they were in luck. The player the girls had their eyes on was busy, so no date, and as it turned out they weren't old enough to drink at Sam's. Steve had saved some beers from his inventory and the group wound up in Eddie's car under some overpass on a dark Oakland street, downing the warm brews. Eddie was having a good time with his date in the front seat, and Steve in the rear seat was happy because his girl was drinking beer faster than he could, which was a real feat. Steve was trying to remove Debbie's blouse when suddenly she began to vomit all over him. "Open the door!" Eddie shouted, but it was too late. Steve was soaked in puke, as was the entire back seat. The disgusting episode put a quick end to the evening. They returned the girls to their car and the date was over. Eddie drove to a self-serve car wash and made Steve clean himself off, along with the backseat.

Working at the Coliseum was done on an as-needed basis by the boss, Big Jim. Big Jim stood outside on the concourse and pointed to the few chosen ones he deemed acceptable to work that particular day. Think of the character "Johnny Friendly" from *On The Waterfront* and you'll have a good idea what Big Jim and the working conditions were like. Steve said he was Mafia, and I don't think he was exaggerating. If he wasn't, he certainly looked the part. If you didn't want to work on a particular night you just didn't show up. Of course, if you did that often enough, they would stop hiring you. Steve would take off almost at will and he did often unless it was a big game, which meant a big paycheck.

One night Steve skipped a big game to go see Woody Allen, who was performing at the Circle Star Theater in nearby San Carlos. Steve had followed his career from the beginning, so he snatched up a ticket immediately. He brought along a still so he could get Woody's autograph. After the show Steve ran backstage, and then kept running—the place was enormous. He ran down empty corridors searching in vain for the famed comedian. Steve kept asking people where the dressing room was, but they all seemed to send him in different directions. Finally, just by luck, he found Mr. Allen coming out of a room. Steve could barely talk, he was panting so much. He approached the comic and said, "Mr. Allen, I'm a big fan. I came all the way from Oakland."

"On foot?" Woody asked.

Steve explained that he did arrive by car, and asked him for the autograph. Woody responded and signed his still. Upon arriving back home he promptly framed the still and hung it on his wall.

The great thing about vending was that you only had to work a few hours and the pay was good, even better than good if it was a well-attended event. The best events were the football games. I soon found out that the crowd at the ballpark could get rowdy, and the football fans were the worst. One Sunday afternoon at a football game I spotted Steve under the bleachers beating the hell out of some guy. The poor bastard was lying prone on the ground as Steve knelt above him, smashing his fist into the guy's face. "He wouldn't pay for his beer" was Steve's only explanation.

We sold two brands of beer: the premium beer was Budweiser and the regular beer was switched between off-brands no one had ever heard of before, let alone tasted. Well, this one night Steve was chosen to sell an off-brand, which was a slap in the face to someone who had worked there as long as he had. You also made less money, since the off-brands were sold at a cheaper price. He must have pissed off the boss again—he knew better than to flirt with the guy's daughter, but the boss must have heard something about one of his antics and handed down the demotion. Only the drunks would buy the off-brands, so Steve hatched a plan. He would carry around an empty Budweiser bottle and wave it to the crowd so they could see the label, implying that he was selling Bud. If someone would ask what type of beer he sold, he would show them the bottle of Bud and smile. When one of Steve's customers spit out the beer he had just purchased and yelled, "This ain't Bud, I want my money back," Steve refused and the irate fan took a swing at Steve, missing. A big mistake. Steve took a better swing and connected, leaving the guy flat on the steps, motionless. It's amazing how many people took a punch at Steve through the years, considering his size and athleticism. *Why try to antagonize the guy?* I thought.

Steve would keep a beer cup in his case just for himself. He became adept at pouring a cup of beer overly quickly, filling the cup mostly with foam, selling the foaming beer to an unsuspecting customer, and then keeping the rest of the beer for himself to enjoy. He always gave a lot of thought to how to pull something over on someone, be it the boss, a customer or whoever. Like baseball, it was a game to him … and he was good at it.

Being so close to beer, drinking his wares became a nightly occurrence. As much as he drank, he rarely showed signs of being drunk. Playful and charming, yes; but drunk, no. It amazed me how he could drink so much and yet show so few signs of inebriation. I think the doctors call it tolerance, but I just thought Steve was invincible.

With plenty of free beer, easy cash, and easier women, Steve became very comfortable with his part-time job. With his devil-may-care personality, good looks, and charm, he even started to become somewhat of a local celebrity, especially in the various bars around the Bay Area. It got to the point that you could mention his name in a bar and more often than not someone there knew him. If it was a woman, they probably slept with him. It would also start to have some repercussions.

I was going to give him a ride home one night from the Coliseum. As we walked to my car I noticed he had been scratching his crotch. "What the hell are you doing?" I asked.

"Damn it, I have crabs and they itch like hell!"

I told him flatly, "You're not riding in my car with crabs." That started an argument. We yelled back and forth for a minute or so and then we compromised. I'd give him a ride but he had to sit on newspapers, and then take the newspapers with him when he left. I told him to burn the papers. He thought I was overreacting.

When we weren't working baseball, basketball, ice hockey, or football games, the rock concerts were the best. During the summer they held Days on the Green concerts at the Coliseum. They were produced by Bill Graham, a famous promoter from San Francisco. The concerts featured such iconic bands as The Who, The Rolling Stones, Jefferson Airplane, Fleetwood Mac, and Peter Frampton, sometimes all on the same bill. It was an amazing time for music and we had a front-row seat.

During one of his introductions, Graham touted other concerts he was putting on around the Bay Area. He mentioned names of famous rock groups and the crowd erupted in cheers. He then named some non-rock performers, including performers from the new so-called "punk" movement. The crowd turned on Graham and booed him. They even booed him when he mentioned jazz performers. I was in shock. Graham announced to the crowd, "You should open your minds to all types of music. Rock is great but expand your horizons. Search out all types of music." Truer words were never spoken at a rock concert. The crowd didn't buy it, though; they kept booing and stomping their feet.

Graham was wise enough to ban beer sales, so Steve and I were relegated to selling frozen chocolate malts. The crowd was so stoned that they really didn't need the booze. While walking into work one morning we saw a young girl waiting in line collapse right in front of us. She fell right on her face, out cold, and hadn't even made it in the door yet. We assumed that the drugs she had taken kicked in a bit earlier than expected.

If a girl asked for a free malt, Steve would ask her for a kiss. ("A good one!") He frequently got it. If the kiss was a really good one, he would ask for a date after the concert … sometimes right after the concert, in his car in the parking lot. During one concert we were chosen to sell T-shirts out of a van after the show ended. Steve was inside tossing out the shirts, while Eddie and I stood at the wooden table selling and collecting the money. When the fans left the stadium we were swamped with customers. We had shirts from all the bands who had performed, but all the requests seemed to be for Blue Öyster Cult. None of us had ever heard of them before, but the audience filing out of the concert was screaming to buy the T-shirts. This must have been one of their first appearances, and we ran low on stock quickly. Steve had a couple of bright business ideas. First, he jacked up the prices. The shirts sold for $10, but he raised them to $15. A fan complained that the other truck was selling them for less. Steve explained, "They're selling the cheap shirts. Ours are made much better. They're higher quality." People believed his lies. When we started to run low on medium shirts, he had another idea. He ripped the tags off the shirts so you couldn't tell the size. We sold the large ones as medium. There was another complaint: "This shirt is too big!" Steve's reply was quick and to the point: "Wash it in hot water, they shrink to fit."

We quickly sold out of our shirts and made a fortune, and this was in addition to the money we had made selling malts. There was only one thing to do. Head to the casinos in Lake Tahoe and Reno, hit the blackjack tables, and make even more money.

THE GAMBLER

No film had a greater influence on Steve prior to 1974 than *Slither* with James Caan. He wore a flat cap just like the one Caan wore, kept his hair curly and short just like Caan, and even went so far as to use Caan's same voice inflections, with the notable exception of his laugh, which Steven took from Burt Reynolds. Steve and Caan nearly looked like twins; equal parts tough and cool.

Two movies released in 1974 had an enormous impact on Steve's life: *The Gambler*, another James Caan film, and *California Split* with Elliott Gould and George Segal. Both films told the story of gamblers who lost everything. But Steve paid no mind to the movies' overarching message; instead, he fell in love with the thrill of playing the odds. He would adopt Caan's dress in *The Gambler*, a denim shirt with the top three buttons unbuttoned to reveal his chest and switch up his flat cap for a baseball cap. (I'm not certain which film influenced that move.) And of course, he'd mimic the lingo from the films, which in the case of *California Split* really pissed off me and most of our friends. Steve was about the only person I knew who enjoyed the Robert Altman film. Perhaps famed film critic Pauline Kael too, as she always championed those types of movies.

One weekend when Steve was on his gambling kick, I joined him and two other friends (Eddie and Benny) for a trip to Reno, which was a four-hour straight shot from Oakland over the Sierra Nevada. We were all flush with cash from a recent rock concert at the Coliseum and hungry for some action. Benny also worked at the ballpark, but rarely joined us on our gambling jaunts. He was several years older, maybe a decade, and he was also a bookie. He did well in his trade, I was told, and he didn't hide it either. I can remember seeing his pockets full of cash. He was generous and had a great sense of humor, making him just about the perfect person to accompany to a bar. Plus, he always seemed to take Steve's ribbing about his Japanese heritage in stride. It was not uncommon for Steve to yell at him over some trivial argument with the epithet, "You Jap bastard, we taught you a lesson in World War II, and if you don't shut the fuck up I'll teach you another lesson now!" As mean-spirited as that kind of talk sounds today, it was commonplace among our group of friends. Benny never let it bother him, at least as far as I could tell, as he would fire back with something about Italians being wop bastards and gangsters.

As I said, Benny was very good-natured, but on the occasions he suffered a big loss, he could disappear in the blink of an eye. I can remember him being gone for days and sometimes weeks at a time. When he returned there would be no mention of where he'd been or what had happened, but I assumed everyone had been paid off. A year or so later, Benny disappeared for good. We all figured that this time he couldn't pay his debts. We never did hear if he was alive or dead. He simply disappeared. He was a fun guy to have around. We all missed him.

The four-hour drive from Oakland to the casinos was an adventure in and of itself. If Steve was driving it would be fast, and it could get crazy. I hated sitting in the back seat when he was behind the wheel. He had this annoying habit of having to face you when he spoke to you. While driving 90 mph on the freeway, he would whip his head around to the person sitting in the backseat and carry on a conversation. Yelling something appropriate like, "Turn the fuck around and watch the damn road!" sometimes worked, but not always, especially if he was drinking. Steve would suck on a beer while driving, keeping the bottle hidden in a brown paper bag. When he emptied the bottle he'd shout, "Give me another bag juice!" One of us would comply and he'd keep on driving. Sometimes on those trips to Reno, the backseat would fill up with so many empty beer bottles that you'd think someone emptied the trash can from a bar in there.

On one trip to Reno, Steve had a bright idea. "Let's smoke some of Eddie's weed," he said with authority. "We'll get the munchies, then go to an all-you-can-eat buffet. We'll fill up with enough food that we won't have to eat for the rest of the trip."

Unfortunately, Eddie had the dope, but no rolling papers. We checked out a couple of liquor stores, but we couldn't find anything. We split into teams and went on our quest—still nothing. It turned out there was an ordinance against selling rolling papers in the city of Reno. So Eddie had the idea to purchase a pack of cigarettes, remove the tobacco and replace it with dope. As difficult as this sounds, it worked.

After smoking Eddie's spliff, we wound up at the buffet inside the Money Tree casino, hungry as only four young stoned guys could be. Eyes beet red, we ate to our stomachs' content. Unfortunately, it would be our last meal for quite some time, as we proceeded to go on a run of bad luck; 24 hours later, we were broke. Between us, we had maybe $3, not even enough to buy gas for the trip home. Steve solved that problem. He drove into a gas station, filled his tank, then in a flash drove off without paying. It was not long after this that gas stations switched to a pay-first policy; I could see why. Steve had another solution for our hunger problem. He stopped at a Taco Bell on the outskirts of Reno and, using his considerable charm, talked the young girl behind the counter into giving us free soft drinks and a large bag of broken taco shells. She seemed genuinely sorry that we'd lost all our money, and wished us well. That was our only sustenance for the long, quiet drive back to the Bay.

Generally speaking, Steve was lucky when it came to gambling. He was the only guy I knew who could take his last $10 and turn it into $300 or $400 (or more) in the matter of an hour. As the saying goes, "Scared money don't make money," and Steve was never scared. He didn't seem to ever fear the consequences, always assuming he'd find a way to get the money back. Unlike most amateur gamblers, the ones who lose more often than they win and go home angry and depressed over their losses, Steve would keep incredibly cool under pressure. If he busted out and lost all his money, he'd ask a buddy for more and just keep on playing. If he was on a losing streak, I knew enough to keep away so that he wouldn't ask me for cash. If he was on a winning streak, he could be very generous with his winnings.

During one particularly successful trip to Lake Tahoe, Steve won enough to treat Eddie, Benny, and himself to a night at Mustang Ranch, the famous brothel a few dusty miles outside of Reno. "Whores and drinks for my buddies!" he drunkenly shouted upon entering. Steve let the guys pick out one hooker each. He then negotiated the "group rate" and paid for the pleasure with a wad full of cash he had rolled up in his front pocket. After having their fun, the three met in the ranch's small bar, where Steve picked up the tab for several rounds of top-shelf liquor. These parties were always very expensive; but when Steve was a winner, he wanted to share his good fortune and keep the good times going for as long as possible.

A few weeks after the Reno bash Steve and Eddie were back at the casinos, this time at Harrah's in Lake Tahoe. This time it was Eddie who was the lucky one. He hit a keno ticket for some big money, almost $2,000. It was the most money he'd ever won in his life. Given his generosity during their previous trip, Steve assumed Eddie would reciprocate and spring for another trip to the whorehouse. Eddie flat-out refused. Steve then pleaded with Eddie to front him some money so he could continue gambling. Eddie refused again. He wouldn't give Steve a dime. Tension built and it turned ugly. They marched outside to the parking lot, started yelling at each other, and eventually punches flew. Eddie was a foot shorter than Steve, so he couldn't do much except try and protect himself from the onslaught. Steve went wild, punching his friend furiously.

A bystander came upon the scene and screamed for help, drawing the attention of several security guards who finally broke it up. No charges were filed since they told the cops they were friends. Eddie was so pissed that he decided to drive home and leave Steve stranded. But being stranded was second nature to Steve. A call to me or some other friend would usually get him bus fare via wire transfer. If he couldn't find someone to bail him out, Steve would beg a bus driver to let him ride for free, or if that didn't work he would just sneak on a bus. There was always a way out of any situation when Steve was involved. Eddie later explained to me that the reason he didn't give Steve the cash was that he was heavily in debt. He had to use all his winnings to bail himself out of a dire situation. He also said, "If I loan Steve money and he loses it, it might be weeks or months before I see it again." He apparently knew Steve as well as I did.

One summer, for some reason I will never understand, Harrah's Casino decided to issue Steve a credit card with a $10,000 limit. Not a wise business move on their part. Steve explained that the card made him feel like James Bond in *Diamonds Are Forever* (although Bond carried a Playboy card in the film, but I guess it was close enough for him). Immediately upon receiving the card we were back in Lake Tahoe. Steve was "On top of the world, Ma," with that card in his pocket. He did well the entire trip, up $1,000 or more. But just about the time we were supposed to pack it in and head home, I found Steve at the blackjack table surrounded by stacks of multi-colored chips.

"Steve, you have plenty of money, it's time to go home," I urged him.

He looked at me incredulously. "Give me a half an hour and I'll be ready," he said.

I told him I would grab something to eat then come right back for him. I wanted to get on the road before nightfall. I hated driving down that godforsaken mountain in darkness. He agreed, then asked the dealer to send the cocktail waitress back over. I toyed with the idea of putting some of his chips in my pocket for safekeeping. He'd been drinking so much I doubt he would have noticed. But I didn't; they were his chips, and they were his responsibility.

Upon my return I found Steve at the same table, only now he was completely smashed and his chips were completely gone. I thought that maybe he had cashed in and most of the money was stuffed in his pocket, but I was wrong. "What happened?" I asked in shock. But he just muttered something back unintelligible. Suffice to say he was now ready to depart. We walked back to the car, exchanging no words. Steve was wobbling back and forth from all the booze. Once inside the vehicle, he fastened the seat belt and quickly passed out. He slept for about an hour until we happened to be driving through Placerville when he jolted awake.

"I just realized what I did..." he groaned. "I lost over $3,000! Why didn't you make me leave?" I had no idea that he had lost so much money.

It wasn't many more trips later before he had maxed out his Harrah's credit card. Since there was no chance of him paying off the debt, he just decided not to even try. "I just won't go back to Tahoe," he said. "They won't come down here looking for me for a lousy ten grand. That's nothing to them. They have millions. Lots of people owe them more money than I do." I was disappointed with his decision but not completely surprised.

Months went by. When the credit card statements from Harrah's arrived, he would simply toss them into the trash. Eventually, the statements stopped arriving and he figured they had just given up and wrote off the debt. I figured the same. *Hell, they're rich, why pick on Steve?* Then one day he received a telephone call from a very serious sounding man. After listening to what the man said, he slammed down the phone and immediately gave me a call. Steve sounded frightened, "John, some guy from a collection agency just called me. They're coming to my apartment at 5 p.m. on Tuesday and demanded to be paid in full … or else." Well, I certainly didn't have the money to lend him. Steve thought they might kill him, or at the very least break his legs, and without the use of his legs he wouldn't be able to sell beer. We had both seen enough mob movies to know what happens when you don't pay off your marker. In a panic, he called other friends, but no one had that kind of cash. Frantic, and with only a few hours remaining, Steve was sweating and desperate. His friends knew the possible outcome, but $10,000 was just too much to ask for, and it was beginning to look hopeless. Finally, in a last-ditch effort, he went to his father. They hadn't spoken in months. The last time they had talked it quickly turned into a fistfight, with The Old Man taking a couple of swings at Steve. Steve didn't want to deck him again, so he just left the house and hadn't returned since.

With his tail between his legs, Steve begged for the money. The Old Man knew the collection guys meant business. He didn't have the funds either, but he could borrow them, and he did. So when the knock came at Steve's apartment door a few days later he had the money, cash in hand. He quickly gave it over. The two guys told him to never ignore a bill from a casino again. Steve had learned his lesson.

The loan from his father wasn't easy to payback. Steve was now broke more often than not. Every cent he made went into paying The Old Man off. It even led him to do the unthinkable: He brought some of his old comic books to a store in San Francisco's Fisherman's Wharf and sold them for cash. He had been saving them for years. He didn't sell his whole collection, not yet anyway, but a substantial portion. It had to hurt.

A few weeks later, after paying off The Old Man, he was back in Tahoe drinking and gambling again. Driving home alone late one night he was pulled over by the Nevada Highway Patrol for speeding. While the cop was writing the ticket, the officer noticed an empty bottle of beer on the floor of the back seat. He confiscated the bottle and wrote him up for an open container as well. Steve was no stranger to tickets, but he would beat them on a regular basis. As a matter of fact, he made beating tickets into something of an art form. His most popular method of beating a ticket was to keep postponing the trial. A postponement meant the police officer who had written the original citation would have to reschedule his court time since he also had to be present. In those days you were typically allowed one request for a delay, but Steve would come up with a heart-tugging sob story, something highly dramatic like that his father had just died and he had to leave town, or some other whopping lie, and they would always buy it. When I heard the calls he made to the court, he was so convincing even I would believe him. He was that sincere. After a few postponements, the cop would give up on appearing. No cop, no case. Once when the cop did show up in court, it had been so long since the incident that he didn't even recognize Steve and had forgotten the specifics of what happened. Again, case dismissed. On that rare occasion when he was sentenced to traffic school, he would pay me or some other friend to take the classes for him. He would, however, always attend the final class so that he could take the final exam. No one ever caught on to this ploy. A traffic judge once shook his head at Steve and told him in a stern voice, "You're just Moses on wheels." We were never quite sure exactly what the judge meant by that, but Steve took it to mean some kind of compliment, repeating it endlessly for all to hear. To Steve it was a badge of honor: "I'm Steve Monzelli, Moses on wheels!"

Steve took me with him to Tahoe when he was finally ordered to appear on the open container charge. I was to be his insurance in the event that he was sentenced to jail time because I could drive his car back to the Bay Area and pick him up when he was released. I was also to lie/explain to his father and his boss at the Coliseum that he was staying in Tahoe a few extra days. "Tell him I'm on a winning streak," Steve told me.

As we sat in the courtroom, we watched the judge sentence driver after driver to incredibly harsh sentences, for what seemed to us as rather minor infractions. Some poor guy was sentenced to jail for having snow covering the back window of his car. Steve had entered the courtroom with all the confidence of Steve McQueen, cool and confident. It was all fading fast. Now he was downright nervous, as I was, and I had nothing whatsoever to do with the case. Defendant after defendant was quickly sentenced and then hauled off by the bailiff. Now it was Steve's turn to stand in front of the judge. Steve had his story well-rehearsed. "Your honor, I had stopped for lunch and ate a sandwich and drank one bottle of beer. There was no garbage can around, and I hate litter so I tossed the trash in the back of my car and forgot about it." The judge stared at Steve and told him, "Next time find a garbage can." Miraculously, the judge bought the bullshit story and dismissed the case.

I can remember another trip when Steve brought a woman named Jena with him for some gambling in Reno. He had been dating her for a few months and was quite taken by her. She was almost as tall as Steve, a striking and wild-looking redhead. She seemed to love Steve and Steve loved her, but the idea of remaining faithful to one woman was a ridiculous concept to him. He was nonetheless grateful to her for introducing several sexual practices that had been foreign to him prior to their courtship. He excitedly told me once, "This girl puts ice cream in her pussy! It tastes great that way! I had no idea!" He was concerned over one of her requests, however. She had asked Steve for anal sex. Worried, Steve confided to a friend that he thought Jena thought he was gay for even asking.

After a few days of heavy gaming, copious amounts of alcohol, and hot sex, the couple headed home. Jena was drinking a cup of hot chocolate during the drive and after a while lost interest. She tossed it out the window and the dark-brown liquid splashed along the side of Steve's always immaculately clean white 1968 Mustang Fastback. Jena put the seat back and took a nap while Steve drove the rest of the way back to Oakland. After an hour or so, Steve noticed a California Highway Patrol car behind him, its lights blazing. For once Steve was not speeding and he could not figure out why he was being stopped. He pulled to the shoulder and opened the door to get out. The officer had his service revolver pointed at Steve and he yelled for him to halt and raise his hands. Knowing he did nothing wrong, Steve continued to walk toward the officer. "Halt!" the officer yelled. "Hands up!" This time Steve listened. The officer threw Steve to the ground and frisked him. Steve begged for an explanation. The officer responded, "You have a dead girl in the car."

Steve yelled out, "Dead? She's sleeping, you fool." The officer had a look for himself. He yelled at Jena, but she didn't move. He yelled again and still nothing. The officer reached into the car, grabbed her shoulder, and shook her, and she finally woke up. She was out cold, due in no small part to not sleeping the night before and having a prodigious hangover. It turned out that some long-haul truck driver had seen the dried hot chocolate on the side of Steve's car and mistaken it for dried blood. That same driver noticed Jena lying motionless in the reclined passenger seat and figured she had been murdered. The trucker radioed the CHP for what he thought was a murder victim in transit. The officer told Steve he had been only seconds away from being shot, and that if he's ever pulled over again to always listen to the commands of the officer. Steve did have one more thing to explain; he had a blood-soaked white pillowcase in the back seat that contained a mannequin head also covered with blood. The explanation was simple … for Steve, that is. The blood was fake stage blood and the pillowcase and head were his tribute to the Sam Peckinpah film, *Bring Me the Head of Alfredo Garcia.* See the film and you'll understand.

While in Lake Tahoe one day, I noticed an article in a local newspaper that John Wayne would be shooting his latest film in nearby Carson City. Wayne was an extremely polarizing figure at this point in history. He was one of the few Hollywood hawks, and as such was considered a right-wing fossil by most. The Vietnam War was still fresh in everyone's memory, and besides that, we were living in one of the most liberal areas in the nation. Anti-war rallies were an almost daily occurrence. No one in our group would admit to being a John Wayne fan, but you did have to give the actor credit for being an iconic figure in film history. When I mentioned the impending filming to Steve, he jumped at the chance to visit the set. It was the perfect opportunity for Steve to show Wayne the photo they took together many years earlier, and have another up-to-date photo taken.

The following week we headed back to Nevada. The location was easy to find. We drove into downtown Carson City and noticed a billboard on the Ormsby House, a huge hotel in the center of the main drag. The billboard read, "We welcome the cast and crew of *The Shootist*." We went into the hotel, checked into the production office, and simply asked them where they were shooting. They told us it was within walking distance. Nevada's capital city, at least in those days, didn't need much prep to look like a scene from the 1880s. The location was on a side street. They were filming in and around an old house, which in the film is owned by a character played by Lauren Bacall. The company had spread dirt on the asphalt streets and added some horse-drawn carriages going up and down it. It sure looked authentic to our eyes. As fate would have it, Bacall had co-starred in *Blood Alley* with Wayne, *Blood Alley* being the location of Steve's first photo-op with the famous actor. Steve clutched the photo next to him, eager to show it to The Duke.

Wayne might have been *persona non grata* in the San Francisco Bay Area, but deep in Nevada, he was a treasured icon. There were hordes of people wanting a glimpse of him. This shocked and surprised us. Wayne's last few films had been turkeys such as *Rooster Cogburn, Brannigan,* and *McQ*. While we dutifully waited behind the ropes to catch a glimpse of him, they called the day a wrap, and the crew started to close the set down. We did catch a look at him briefly, surrounded by a group of people, waving to the crowd as he was put into a car and driven away. We had planned to stay a couple of days, so perhaps we would have better luck tomorrow, we thought. We did notice director Don Siegel walking alone, back to his car. Siegel was one of our favorites. He directed such films as *Dirty Harry, The Lineup,* and one of the greatest films of all time, *Invasion of the Body Snatchers*. I had a striking still of him directing *Dirty Harry*, so we rushed over and asked him if he would autograph it. He gladly did. I wondered later just how often he received that request. He seemed really pleased that we knew his work and answered our few questions before getting into his car and driving off. We felt he enjoyed our brief encounter. John Wayne was the star of the film, but Don Siegel was the star to us because he had created so many of our favorite movies.

Later that night, we went to a casino to try our luck. As happened often, I tapped out early. I just couldn't seem to win; I either didn't know how to gamble or had the worst luck in the world. I should have learned my lesson. Steve might have lost many more times than he won, but he did win, before eventually losing his money. I never seemed to win at any point.

The next day on the set we ran into Chuck Roberson. 'Bad Chuck' as he was known had been John Wayne's stunt double for years. He was kind enough to fill us in on his career and tell us stories about working with Wayne, John Ford, and many others. We showed him the photo of Steve and Wayne. He explained to us that Wayne was a busy fellow and that it was best to leave him alone while he was working. Bad Chuck posed for a few photos and seemed like a nice guy. He eventually told us we should go to the production office after filming wrapped, that Wayne just might check-in for a few minutes. We gladly did as we were told. We showed someone in the office the photo but they seemed less than impressed. I showed the guy my still of Wayne and asked if I could have it signed. The guy snapped back with, "What do I look like, an autograph service?" He did tell me reluctantly that I could leave the still with him, along with my address, and he would see what he could do. Unfortunately, we never did get the chance to meet up with The Duke, let alone show him the photo with baby Steve, the photo Steve proudly carried with him during our stay in Carson City.

A few weeks after we returned home, my autographed still of Wayne arrived in the mail. I was truly grateful that they did become an autograph service, for me that is. It was a still from the film *The Fighting Kentuckian,* and it showed Wayne and co-star Oliver Hardy. It was boldly inscribed, "To John, Good Luck, John Wayne." It meant a lot.

When filming wrapped in Carson City, the cast and crew returned to Warner Bros. in Burbank to complete the production. Wayne became ill, which delayed the end of filming. For a while it looked like the movie might not get finished. Rumor had it that Wayne had cancer again, just like his character in the film. The movie was eventually completed and became one of the actor's great films. It was also his last feature; Wayne died in 1979, two years after completing it.

GOING PLACES

What better place than Hollywood could there possibly be for a couple of film buffs? Los Angeles is a five-hour drive from the Bay Area; and fortunately for us, Steve had an aunt and uncle who lived in Huntington Beach, which was only about a 30-minute drive from Hollywood. We had stayed with them briefly before, during our trip to Disneyland, and it was a good deal for all. We wouldn't have to spend a dime for a motel room, and Steve's Aunt Peg and Uncle Jimmy loved our company. Aunt Peg was The Old Man's sister; fortunately, she shared none of his loud, obnoxious character traits.

Since Steve had lived in L.A. as a young boy and had visited frequently with his parents and brother, he sort of knew his way around. One part of town he knew exceptionally well was Hollywood Boulevard—the street of dreams, a movie lover's mecca. At stores like Collectors Bookstore, Bond Street Books (on Wilcox Avenue, just off Hollywood), Larry Edmunds Bookshop, and many more, one could find an endless trove of posters, lobby cards, press books, and stills, all sorts of film paraphernalia. These businesses were everywhere, up and down the boulevard. What little money we had in our pockets, we spent on all the movie memorabilia we could find. It was a fantastic time to be a collector. Movie posters at this time were, for the most part, considered trash. You could find them, even those from the earliest days of Hollywood, for a very reasonable price. During our first trip, we spent the day searching for film treasures and then headed back to Aunt Peg and Uncle Jimmy's for the night.

They lived in your typical small stucco Southern California post-World War II home. Friends and acquaintances would drop in and stay all the time, almost like it was a bed and breakfast, sans the breakfast. We never knew who was going to be there or when they would show up. Neither, it seemed, did Peg and Jimmy. Friends, family, friends of family, and near-strangers would pop by constantly. One night when I was fast asleep on the floor in my sleeping bag, an unknown woman came into the room, turned on a night light, and undressed. I awoke in time to see her check herself out in a full-length mirror, put on a change of clothes, turn off the light, and exit. The next morning I could barely contain my excitement and told Steve about it. I thought since he was using the bed he must have slept through it, but he'd seen the whole show as well. We talked about it the entire day, hoping beyond hope that she would come back that night. She did not. We never did find out who she was, but we always held out hope that she would one day return.

Aunt Peg was a wonderful cook. She made amazing Italian food, with tastes I'd never experienced. Both she and Uncle Jimmy gladly shared wine with me and Steve, with no thought given to me being underage. I knew enough not to abuse the wine; I drank it with dinner and never after. It was a joy eating at her dining table. Uncle Jimmy loved to invite people over to eat; but unfortunately for Aunt Peg, the guests were often his buddies from the bar. They came by after closing, needing a bite to eat and, more often than not, a little more to drink. This perturbed Aunt Peg, but no begging on her part would stop Uncle Jimmy from his almost nightly post-bar ritual.

One evening, after Jimmy had rustled her out of bed at 2 a.m. demanding food for his drunken buddies, she'd had enough. Thoroughly pissed off, she thought up a plan to get even. She cooked hamburgers for the gang. When they were finished devouring them, she asked them what they thought. All nodded in approval, agreeing they had been some tasty burgers. Then she told them her secret ingredient: "You're all eating fried dog food … and that's all I'm cooking from now on!" One of the drunken guests vomited on the floor immediately upon hearing the news. The rest ran out the door, yelling at Jimmy. Aunt Peg's plan worked like a charm. Word of her special late-night treat spread rapidly at the bar. From that moment on, at closing, no one ever wanted to go over to Jimmy's house again.

Before our next trip to L.A., we had the idea to locate the homes of movie stars and drop by and ask for autographs. The addresses were easy enough to find in those days; the Who's Who in the local public library was loaded with them. I also found the City of Los Angeles telephone book. It was amazing how many celebrities were listed in there. I was working in a movie theater at the time and my boss, who was also a big movie fan, turned out to be a great source of information. He always seemed to know who was at the Motion Picture & Television Country House and Hospital in Calabasas, and which actor we should visit as soon as possible lest they pass away.

During our many trips to Los Angeles, we knocked on the doors of as many luminaries as possible. One afternoon we went to the home of James Stewart, who was about 65 at the time. We rang the doorbell, waited, and then rang it a few more times. It took a long while but the cinema icon eventually answered; we couldn't believe it. The thick door opened slowly and in an apologetic way he explained that he had been in the backyard working in his garden. He was very pleasant, albeit surprised to find two strangers at his door. He acted like no one had ever just dropped by before to say "Hi." We mentioned that we had just come from Raymond Massey's house and that he had slammed the door in our face. Stewart looked surprised and said, "I had no idea Raymond Massey lived so close." I thought that was strange.

I figured all the actors in the area would certainly know each other. Stewart kindly signed our stills and sent us on our way. As fate would have it, the very next day I found a great still from *Mr. Smith Goes to Washington* while rummaging through boxes at Larry Edmunds Bookshop. It was an original issue from 1939 and hand-tinted. A rare find indeed. I just had to have him sign that one, too. So we drove back to his house and knocked on the door again. When he opened the door and saw us standing on his porch he exclaimed, "Weren't you boys here yesterday?" I piped up. "Yes sir, but I found a better still." He signed the picture but I had the feeling he didn't really want to see us again.

Persistence didn't always pay off. Steve was a big fan of actor James Coburn. We had his Beverly Hills address and Steve just *had* to meet him. Coburn was from the "cool" style of acting, popular in the 1960s. As I wasn't very familiar with his work, I didn't really want to go knocking on Coburn's door; but it was important to Steve, so I went along. We walked up the circular driveway and arrived at what was a modest house by Beverly Hills standards. I rang the doorbell. The woman who answered the door appeared to be a housekeeper, or maybe an assistant. We gave her our normal spiel: "We're huge fans of Mr. Coburn's, we came all the way from the San Francisco Bay Area, could he sign some stills for us?" She informed us that Mr. Coburn was not at home, and even if he was, he wouldn't want to see us. Steve asked if we could leave the stills and if she could she get them autographed and send them to us. To my shock and surprise, she agreed. She took down our address, grabbed the photos, and closed the door.

It was during one of our later trips to L.A. that it dawned on Steve, "James Coburn never sent our stills back to us!" This infuriated him, especially since he was such a big fan. "Let's go get our stills back," he said. So back we drove to Coburn's home. This had to be four or five months later. Steve rang the doorbell and the same woman answered.

Steve blurted out, "We left some stills here for James Coburn to autograph and we never received them. They're really important to us." The woman came back with, "I remember you two. I had Mr. Coburn sign them and I sent out the stills myself. They should be at your home sometime soon." This satisfied Steve; he thanked the woman and off we went. Back home we waited and waited but they never arrived. We went back to Los Angeles many times, but Steve never mentioned going back for a third try to Coburn's home. Steve was not one to give up, but I don't recall another mention of this.

At the time, the early '70s, Alfred Hitchcock was the most famous director living. He made his home on a sprawling estate on Bellagio Drive in Beverly Hills. Somehow we got the address and figured he would be the perfect person to visit. We knew all his movies. *North by Northwest* seemed to be playing in every revival theater in the Bay Area, and we rarely missed an opportunity to see it, or any of his other classic thrillers. We easily located Hitchcock's home and parked on the street, only a few yards from his driveway. Since this was the era before gated estates, we never had a problem getting access to someone's front door. Steve and I, proudly armed with our vast film knowledge and a couple of publicity stills, walked down his driveway, admiring the vast green lawn as we made our way to the front door. As we both stood on his porch, we took a deep breath and then knocked. An English housekeeper answered the door, stared at us, and curtly asked, "What do you two want?"

Steve, always the bold one, spoke up. "We're fans of Mr. Hitchcock's and we would like him to autograph some stills for us."

The housekeeper was flabbergasted. "This is Mr. Hitchcock's private home! If you have business with him, go to the studio!" With that, she closed the door, loudly. It was strange, I thought. She too acted like no one ever just drops by to say hello.

"What a great idea!" Steve said as we walked away from the house. "Let's go see him over at Universal!" Hitchcock had had an office at Universal Studios for years. The studio wasn't very far away, so we jumped in the car and drove to Universal City. I had only been on the tour once previously, and that was when I was 11 or 12. For the price of admission, we were now being driven around world-famous Universal Studios (okay, along with dozens of others inside a tram, not a limousine; at least we were inside the studio). The tram took us to "prop plaza," an area filled with old movie props, like a giant hand and telephone from the classic sci-fi film *The Incredible Shrinking Man*. The tram stopped and we were encouraged to walk around and take photos. Once we disembarked, Steve's plan went into effect. We both snuck away from the group and walked down the hill toward Hitchcock's office. The tour guide had helpfully pointed out the location to our group just a few minutes before. With my envelope containing a great portrait of Hitchcock in my hand, we entered the office.

"We would like to meet Mr. Hitchcock," we announced to the women seated behind the desk. The woman could have been the sister of Hitchcock's housekeeper. She told us, "You just don't enter Mr. Hitchcock's office. You must have an appointment to meet him. And besides, he's not in at the moment." She told us he was at a luncheon. From the tone of her voice, we knew better than to show up again unannounced. At least we were lucky that she didn't call security. We left the office with my beautiful unsigned photo still under my arm.

Steve figured that since we were on the lot, we might as well have a look around. Not far from the Hitchcock bungalow we saw an enormous sound stage. I seem to remember it was the famous *Phantom of the Opera* stage. This stage was built for the 1925 version starring Lon Chaney. The outside was lined with trucks and crew members, so we got up close so we could see what they were filming inside. Turns out it was *Midway,* starring Charlton Heston. We stood as close to the action as possible and watched Jack Smight direct a scene with the great Japanese actor Toshiro Mifune. Mifune was standing on a mockup of a destroyer, giving orders to actor James Shigata. They were using water from a firehose and a wind machine to give it some authenticity. *How cool*, we thought at the time. It all looked so real. Steve would have stayed on the lot all day, but I was worried about being caught. I persuaded him to leave, and we finally walked out the employee entrance and up the hill back to the parking lot. We didn't get to meet Hitchcock, but it turned out to be a grand tour nonetheless.

Two other well-known film directors were much easier to track down. At our young age, we were not completely versed in the works of the great Fritz Lang, but we did know he directed *Metropolis*, the classic German silent sci-fi masterpiece, and that was enough for us to want to meet him. His house was on a quiet street off Benedict Canyon Road. The house was a difficult find but, when we did finally locate it, Steve knocked on the door. A young man answered and stared at us. We were not the people he was expecting. Stealing a glance over his shoulder we immediately noticed Lang sitting in a chair near a window that overlooked the canyon. After our normal pitch, the man told us that Lang had been very ill and could not come to the door. Steve, the eternal optimist, responded, "I heard he's getting better."

The guy looked surprised. "He's 85 years old. You don't get better at that age," he said.

Fortunately, he offered to get the photos signed and send them to us. We did as requested but I figured I'd never see my wonderful original still again. *He's going to pull a James Coburn on us*, I thought. Well, surprise of surprises, only a week or so later Lang mailed them back signed. He had even addressed the envelope himself. *What a nice guy*, I thought. It wasn't until the advent of home video, still almost a decade off, that I was finally able to watch Lang's complete filmography on DVD. It was then I realized we had been at the home of a true master of cinema.

On one of these impromptu celebrity home visits, we actually were invited inside. Rouben Mamoulian is perhaps best known for directing the 1932 version of *Dr. Jekyll and Mr. Hyde*, and the first Technicolor feature, *Becky Sharpe*. *Jekyll and Hyde* had just been reissued and was fresh in our memories. It had played on a triple bill at a cinema in San Francisco along with *Mask of Fu Manchu* and *Mark of the Vampire*. Mr. Mamoulian's housekeeper was the one who answered the door, and to our shock and delight, she welcomed us in and took us to the director's library. "Wait here and Mr. Mamoulian will be with you shortly," she said.

It was a magical and almost surreal moment. We were about to meet a famous director who we didn't know, just because we had the gumption to knock on his door. Mr. Mamoulian entered and sat down behind a large desk and seemed very happy to entertain a couple of guests. It all seemed very formal like he thought we might be in the movie business and were there to discuss a project. He was very kind in an old-world formal sort of way. He signed my still and then asked Steve where his photo was. Steve explained that he hadn't been able to find one during our trip to Hollywood. Mamoulian excused himself and left the room, only to return with a still, even better than the one I had found. It was from his film *The Mark of Zorro*. He inscribed it to Steve. I was jealous that he didn't bring one for me, too. Mamoulian didn't know about *Dr. Jekyll and Mr. Hyde* being re-released. He was overjoyed when we told him the audience in San Francisco had loved it. We asked him how the transformations from the kindly Dr. Jekyll to the monstrous Dr. Hyde were achieved. We both knew it was a closely held secret, but we figured maybe he would tell us. He smiled and refused our request. We chatted for 30 minutes or so. *A real classy guy*, I thought. Years later I saw Mamoulian at a tribute at the Academy of Motion Pictures Arts and Sciences in Beverly Hills. I wanted to thank him for being so kind to a couple of young film buffs years earlier. Unfortunately, I wasn't able to get close enough to tell him. Oh, how times had changed.

Steve missed a chance to meet another one of our favorite directors because of yet another day in traffic court. Sam Peckinpah had directed *The Wild Bunch* some five or six years before, but his game-changing Western was still fresh in our minds. I can't begin to remember how many times we watched that film, perhaps 20 or 30. I know this sounds excessive, but we saw this film every chance we could. We knew almost every frame of the film. We quoted from it constantly. Driving down to Los Angeles with my buddy Tom one day, I had noticed that the world-famous Grauman's Chinese Theater was having a sneak preview of Peckinpah's latest film, *Junior Bonner*. Tom and I went to the preview and not only did we meet the great director, but his frequent co-star Warren Oates. We snapped as many pictures at the event as possible. Oates appeared wildly drunk in a couple of the photos, which only made them better. We told the famed director that we were huge fans of his work, and mentioned to him the number of times we'd seen *The Wild Bunch*. He told us that we would like this new film of his, and to be sure to see his upcoming film, *The Getaway*. "It's full of action and gunfights," he told us, which sounded intriguing and thrilling. Steve was due to arrive by plane the following day. When he arrived we told him of our good fortune in meeting Peckinpah and Oates. He didn't believe us; it was just too good to be true. It was a few weeks later, back in the Bay Area, when I showed the photos to him and the gang at Cinema Treasures (Patrick was also a dedicated

Peckinpah fan) that Steve finally believed us and realized what a great event he missed.

Sam Peckinpah at the Grauman's Chinese Theater for the preview of *Junior Bonner*. (Photo by John Gloske)

Warren Oates along with the author (right) and Sam Peckinpah's son Matthew following the preview of *Junior Bonner*.

The Marx Brothers were always one of our favorite comedy teams. During the early '70s, their popularity surged. College campuses and revival theaters screened their films constantly, to wildly enthusiastic crowds. Groucho was living on Hillcrest Drive in Beverly Hills, so we went to see him as well. His cook answered the door. We explained our mission and she was most sympathetic to our cause. She was from Oakland, the city Steve lived in at the time and the city I was born in. She told us that Groucho was not home, but that we could leave our stills with her and she would see that he signed them. As we stood in the breezeway talking to this nice woman, Groucho drove up in his Mercedes. The car stopped only a few feet from us, but Groucho did not get out. He sat there, frozen stiff behind the wheel, looking rather dazed. *Should he be driving?* I thought to myself.

After what seemed like an eternity, Groucho exited very, very slowly. The frail comic icon eyed us with suspicion and asked in a soft voice that was barely above a whisper, "Who are you?"

Before we answered I noticed that both of his shoelaces were untied. Steve spoke up. "We're fans of yours from San Francisco. Would you autograph some stills for us?" Very quietly and weakly he answered, "I'm very tired. I've been rehearsing all day. If you want anything signed, see Erin." Erin Fleming was his companion during the last years of his life. Groucho slowly shuffled off into his house. We left the stills with the cook and picked them up the following day. As promised, they were signed. At the time, we were convinced that we had been some of the last people to see Groucho alive. Due to his frailness, we thought he would die before we could make it back to his home and collect our autographed stills. Surprisingly he kept going; he even performed a one-man show in Los Angeles. We had seen the show performed in San Francisco. It was a sad evening. Groucho read his lines off cue cards and eventually lost his place, becoming confused and bewildered. He kept going but it often made little sense. He should have stayed home. We always want to remember these entertainers as they were in their prime.

If we happened to run out of addresses, there was one place where you could always count on seeing celebrities: The Motion Picture & Television Country House and Hospital, about a 30-minute drive from Hollywood. People who work in the industry pay a percentage of their wages to support the place, and if the need arises they can spend their final years living there for free. It's part hospital and part assisted living facility, all surrounded by beautiful hills. Steve hated visiting the place. "John, you're a ghoul," he was fond of saying. Maybe, but it was the place to find a plethora of our favorite actors and directors before they checked out of this world and into the next. I had been informed by my boss, who always seemed to know who was living there and who we should visit quickly before it was too late, that Larry Fine of *The Three Stooges* was a resident. Armed with yet another beautiful keyset still from one of their shorts, I just had to have him sign it. We easily found his room, and since the door was open we peeked in. There he was, the famed curly-headed member of the prolific comedy team. He was seated in a wheelchair with his head slumped down. He appeared to be sleeping, or worse.

"I'm not going in there!" Steve whispered to me.

I replied, "I have an original key set still. I have to get it signed!"

A woman walking down the hall must have noticed our trepidation. She said to us, "Go in, Larry loves visitors." So we did. After repeating "Hello Mr. Fine" a few times with ever-increasing volume, he awoke. Larry had previously suffered a stroke, but once he was awake he was alert and friendly. We introduced ourselves and told him we had traveled all the way from the Bay Area to see him. He seemed genuinely pleased that we were there. I asked him if Moe ever comes to visit. "Ah, yeah, once in a while," he said. I was hoping beyond hope that maybe Moe would drop by and he could also sign my photo. Fortunately for us, Larry's stroke did not affect his handwriting. I handed him the picture and he wrote, "To John, from your pal, Larry." I told him how much we had enjoyed his movies through the years. Steve finally spoke up and told him, "I'm surprised you still have hair, I would have thought Moe had pulled it all out." That brought a faint smile to his face.

We finally ran out of things to say to him and we figured it was about time to beat it so that he could get some more sleep. As we were about to leave, another woman entered the room, I had a feeling that she was a relative. We explained why we were in the room.

"Thanks so much for visiting Larry," she said. "It really cheers him up." That made Steve feel a little better about the trip.

Since we were already inside the complex, we decided to have a look around and see who else might be in residence. We spotted Jerry Colonna's name on a door. Colonna had been a comedian back in the '40s and had appeared with Bob Hope for years on film, radio, and USO tours. We opened the door to have a look and Colonna laid motionless in his bed. His hair and famous bushy mustache were the same, only pure white. We later learned that he too had suffered a stroke, only a far more serious one than had befallen Larry Fine. As we were about to leave the building, we noticed a door, slightly opened, without a name on it. We peeked in and noticed an elderly man asleep on a bed. "It's John Ford!" I whispered to Steve. Steve pulled me away from the door before I woke the famed director. He wanted to get out of the place quickly; he had seen enough of the ill and elderly motion picture people. On the way back to Huntington Beach, Steve started to have doubts that we had really seen the Academy Award-winning director. He was quiet for most of the ride back and then out of the blue said, "I think it was a good thing that we visited Larry Fine. It made him happy. Maybe you're not a ghoul after all."

We had such a good time during our trips to Los Angeles. I can remember one time while Steve was driving south on Highway 5 as I was pursuing a newspaper, checking out the movie listings. These were the days before most major films had nationwide releases. L.A. was full of tiny theaters showing obscure films; many were grindhouse types that showed foreign films or exploitation triple bills. If you missed the showing at that particular cinema, you might not ever see the film again. I scoured the ads, looking for just these sorts of movies when I ran across an intriguing ad for The Pussycat Theater on Santa Monica Boulevard. "Today at noon, *Deep Throat* star Linda Lovelace will implant her breasts in cement in front of the theater," the ad read. I asked, "It starts in three hours. Can we make it?" It was a stupid question. I knew too well how he drove.

Unfortunately, by the time we arrived at the theater the ceremony was over, but Linda Lovelace was still there in the lobby talking to guests and friends. This time it was Steve who went over and told her just how much he had enjoyed her film. She was so happy with his comment that she gave him a firm hug and kissed him on the lips. Steve was overjoyed. He knew that back at the Coliseum he would be king for a week or more for kissing the most famous porn star on Earth. Once we were back in the car, the kiss was the only thing he could talk about. Growing tired of hearing about it I asked, "Steve, you know what that mouth of hers is famous for?" He thought about it for a few seconds and fell silent.

Tickets to television show tapings were plentiful and normally easy to get. Steve picked up a couple of tickets to *The Diana Rigg Show* that was to be filmed in Studio City, at a studio that was once Republic Studios. Republic made the best serials and was a favorite studio of mine. Steve was jazzed because Diana Rigg had been a co-star of *On Her Majesty's Secret Service*, one of our favorite James Bond films. On the show, Rigg portrayed a tennis pro and spent most of the episode in a sexy tennis outfit. After the filming concluded, we both snuck backstage to meet her and have our stills autographed. She was very happy to meet us and overjoyed when Steve told her she was the best female lead in all the Bond films. She was so pleased with Steve's praise that she gave him a quick hug and a kiss on the cheek. I was extremely jealous that he got the kiss and not me. I told him later that Diana Rigg's kiss canceled out the kiss from Linda Lovelace.

Not all television show tickets were easy to come by. One show, in particular, was very difficult to get into, and that one was *The Tonight Show Starring Johnny Carson*. Since we didn't have tickets, I figured it would be impossible to get into the taping; but as always, Steve had a plan. The audience line stretched down the sidewalk in front of NBC's Burbank studio. "Leave everything to me, I'll get us in," Steve said with confidence. We walked up to the head of the line and spotted a young woman at the door holding a clipboard. Steve greeted her and said, "We're friends of Ted Moore, the cameraman. He reserved two seats for us." The woman checked her clipboard and found no such request. She promptly got on the phone and asked a supervisor what to do. We didn't hear the answer, but in a flash, we were escorted to front row seats to watch the taping. I sat there terrified. Ted Moore was indeed a cinematographer, but he was the cinematographer on the early James Bond films, not *The Tonight Show*. They never did notice their mistake; but because I sat there during the entire show waiting for security to boot us out, I really didn't enjoy the taping.

On occasion, one of our friends would tag along with us to L.A. Willie was one such friend who wanted to join in the fun. Willie had been a friend of mine since high school but knew Steve only vaguely, which meant he didn't know how to deal with him. On the way down to southern California, Willie was sleeping in the back seat of Steve's Barracuda. I was driving and during a long, hot open stretch on Highway 5, Steve grabbed Willie's sneakers and, without a word of warning, tossed them out the window. He did this without malice; he just wanted to liven up the long, boring drive. Willie woke up immediately and realized what had happened. Instead of yelling at Steve and calling him out on his outrageous behavior, he asked in a whiny voice for me to turn around so that he could retrieve his shoes.

Steve was laughing hysterically. I did as Willie requested and somehow he got his footwear back without being killed on the busy highway.

For the rest of the trip, Steve kept harassing Willie. Steve knew he could get to him and he did. While walking around the streets of Hollywood, Willie broke down and cried. It was shocking to see a guy in his early twenties acting this way. I tried explaining to him that he should stand up for himself and give to Steve as good as he got. However, it was not built into him; he wanted to call his mom to come and pick him up. I told him I would talk to Steve and get him off his back. I did, and Steve left him alone, but Steve lost any respect for him, and I didn't see much of Willie after that. If Steve got out of hand, you had to argue your point, and sometimes that meant shouting and threatening. That he respected, not weakness.

SMILE

One afternoon while Steve was sitting around reading the newspaper, a job listing caught his eye. It was from a courier service, promising extensive travel and good pay. "We'll be just like secret agents!" Steve called immediately to say. "We can travel the world *and* get paid for it!" The whole thing sounded shady to me. I was still working at the New Lorenzo movie theater and pretty happy with the arrangement. The theater changed the bill almost weekly, and as an usher I was able to watch almost every film they showed, not to mention consume all the popcorn, soda, and candy I wanted. I didn't want to give that up. Steve decided to go for it. Since he could basically work whenever he wanted to at the Coliseum, picking up a second job was no trouble. The courier company interviewed Steve and did a background check. After a week or so, the results came back: he was in, an official courier. *A courier for what?* he wondered.

His role in the operation was simple enough. He would wait for a phone call giving him a time and terminal location at the San Francisco International Airport. Once inside the airport, a stranger would meet him and handcuff a briefcase to his wrist. He would then hand Steve a roundtrip ticket to a location not previously disclosed, then walk him to the gate to ensure that he boarded the plane. When Steve arrived at his destination, yet another stranger would meet him, remove the handcuffed briefcase, then send him on his way. The job took him to New York City most often, and Florida on occasion. He could stay in the cities he traveled to as long as he wished, but the pay was so low he rarely lingered long before returning home. On one of his Florida stops he met a woman at an airport restaurant and after consuming a few drinks, she took Steve to her house for a night of rousing sex. It must have been extra rousing because he remained in Florida for a couple of weeks. When he finally arrived back in the Bay Area, he told me all that great sex made him feel like a secret agent, albeit an underpaid one. After a few more months of flying back and forth between the coasts, he quit; the thrill of being a "secret agent" had worn off. Ultimately, despite all those assignments, Steve told me he only got laid that one time. Not great odds for a secret agent.

Turned out, Steve had quit his courier job just in time. In the mid to late 1970s, film production was ramping up in the Bay Area. It was our hope to get extra gigs on the films; but if not, at least we could watch them being made. Patrick was our go-to guy for all things film. Not only did he know where the movies were being shot, more often than not he would also know someone involved in the production. Patrick had been breaking out into other endeavors. He was producing a popular television show in San Francisco called *The Worst of Hollywood*. They showed awful "B" films that had fallen into the public domain, most from Patrick's personal collection. The host of the show would provide some background on the films and speak to actors/directors who were connected to them. When they couldn't find a celebrity guest, they would use dubious guests such as Will Rove, a friend of Patrick's who claimed to be Hollywood's Jungle Boy from 1950s television. I was also used as a guest. They were showing an early 1930s Rin Tin Tin movie, and I claimed to be living next door to a dog named Zorro, a distant relative to the Hollywood canine. I went to great lengths to explain what a joy it was to live next door to a relative of a celebrity dog. It was that kind of show, and this was still years before bad films were celebrated in books and documentaries, starting in the late 1970s and continuing into the 1980s. Besides his

Saturday night show, Patrick was also writing screenplays on spec. He would eventually interest producers such as Alan Ladd, Jr. and Michael Wayne (son of John Wayne) in some of his projects.

    If Patrick wasn't aware of a film shooting in the Bay Area, Herb Caen was. Caen was a Pulitzer Prize-winning columnist for the *San Francisco Chronicle,* and his daily piece would frequently mention what shows were being produced locally, giving the exact location and the featured actors. I read the column every day and would keep Steve posted on the news. It was late 1972 when I read in Caen's column about Francis Ford Coppola filming *The Conversation* at the Embarcadero Center. It was Coppola's first film after *The Godfather.* Steve and I walked around the plaza and watched Coppola direct Cindy Williams and Frederic Forrest. From what we could tell, the picture didn't look very interesting. There were no shootouts—and certainly no dead horses—like in *The Godfather.* When the film was released almost two years later, the reviews were excellent and it was eventually nominated for three Academy Awards, including Best Picture and Best Screenplay. We learned our lesson: It's probably best to wait until the film is released before criticizing it.

    In early 1973, Patrick told us that Clint Eastwood was in town filming a sequel to his immensely popular and controversial film, *Dirty Harry.* The sequel was entitled *Magnum Force.* Steve and I had seen Eastwood at a tribute to his work at the San Francisco Film Festival sometime prior, and we were shocked by the jeers and boos he received when *Dirty Harry* came up. Some of the reviews were brutal, calling the film "fascist." Patrick was able to tell us just where they were shooting; it was on a dock just south of the San Francisco-Oakland Bay Bridge. When we showed up, they were filming the finale of the movie. The director was Ted Post, who had recently directed *Beneath the Planet of the Apes.* The crew was relatively small in number and both Post and Eastwood were very approachable. At one point when we noticed the famous actor was on a break, Steve and I approached him and I unfurled my original movie poster from *Francis in the Navy*, Eastwood's second film in which he appeared alongside the famous talking mule. "Mr. Eastwood," I asked, "Would you please autograph my poster for me?"

He looked surprised that anyone would own the poster, let alone want it signed. "I'm not even on the poster!" he laughed.

I told him I realized that, but I really liked the film. He eventually signed it then took it around to show Ted Post and other members of the production crew. They all had a good laugh. In fact, he had it for so long I started to worry he wouldn't give it back. Fortunately, he did. I thanked him for the autograph and then Steve and I told him how shocked we were with his reception at the film festival. He shrugged it off with, "It's San Francisco!" We hung around and watched them film one of the final scenes, but I told Steve that it was bothering me that I didn't have something more significant for Eastwood to sign. After all, he was the number-one box office star at the time.

Steve came up with a solution. We jumped into his car and headed for Cinema Treasures. Patrick sold me a beautiful still from *Dirty Harry*. Once back on the set, I asked Eastwood for one more favor. He happily obliged. We continued to watch them set up a shot involving a car chase and a lot of bullets being fired, fun stuff. While standing around we got into a conversation with Felton Perry, one of the actors in the film. We had never heard of him and we weren't certain what he did in the picture. Perry was nice enough to explain to us exactly what the crew was trying to accomplish during the scene and answer all our questions. We were shocked when we finally saw the finished film because he played Clint Eastwood's partner, something he never mentioned to us on set. I remember thinking what a great guy he was to spend so much time with us.

Francis Ford Coppola directing *The Conversation* in San Francisco. *(Photo by John Gloske)*

Director Ted Post (white hat) and Clint Eastwood on location in San Francisco for the filming of *Magnum Force*. *(Photo by John Gloske)*

Steve heard the amazing news first from Patrick: Richard Burton and Lee Marvin would be filming their new movie, *The Klansman*, in Oroville, a two-and-a-half-hour drive north of San Francisco. Better yet, it was to be directed by Terence Young, who had helmed three of the very best James Bond films. Also in the cast was the gorgeous Italian actress Luciana Paluzzi, co-star of *Thunderball*, and the only woman in all the Bond films to resist Bond's immense charm, refusing to join "the good guys" even after a roll in the hay with 007. Others in the film included David Huddleston, Linda Evans, and making his big-screen debut, O.J. Simpson. Steve was convinced we could land roles in the movie. "John, how many actors could there possibly be in Oroville?" he said. So Steve, Patrick, and I drove to Oroville. Oroville was a rather small, sleepy town, but infamous at the time. Three years earlier, notorious serial killer, Juan Vallejo Corona, was arrested there and convicted of 20 machete murders. Authorities felt he likely killed many more. Upon arriving, Patrick spotted a motel for us to stay in. As I drove into the lot and headed for the manager's office, Patrick told us to stay in the car and that he would take care of the room registration. Upon entering our room that we would be staying in for the next several days, I was shocked to see there was only one bed. "We'll save money this way," Patrick said. "We'll flip coins. Whoever wins the first flip gets the bed frame along with the box springs. The second runner-up gets the mattress on the floor along with one sheet. The loser gets the floor, along with the rest of the sheets, the blankets, and all the pillows." This all made a lot of sense at the time. We quickly separated the mattress and the bedding so that each of us could have our own beds. I, of course, wound up the loser.

Steve offered to go across the street to a diner and pick up some food. He came back with a couple of large boxes of fried chicken and enough six-packs of beer to last us a week (I was not yet 21, but it didn't matter). Within the first hour, the room was in shambles. The bedding was scattered everywhere. Food containers and leftover fried chicken dotted the floor, and at least two six-packs of empty beer cans were lying about. As we sat around downing the brews and watching television, which was on extra loud, there came a knock at the door. I answered it and it was the motel manager. He stuck his head in and, shocked by the condition the room was in, asked to speak with "Mr. James." Patrick apparently had registered under the name of Frank James (as in the outlaw Jesse James' brother). He also registered as one guest, not three. He also gave a phony license plate number for my car. Patrick paid the extra fee for Steve and me and also promised to have the room back in shape before we checked out. And oh yes, we promised to keep the volume down on the TV.

The next day Steve and I checked in with the production office (Patrick had no desire to be an extra), who informed us that they were only going to hire local people and there were plenty of them to choose from. They did take down our contact information, just in case we were needed. *Yeah, right*, I thought. Luckily, we did have an in on the set. Patrick knew co-star Cameron Mitchell. Mitchell had been a customer at Cinema Treasures and struck up a friendship with Patrick. Patrick introduced us to Mitchell, who promptly told us, "This is going to be my comeback picture." His career had hit the skids some years earlier and he had been appearing in so-called "Eurotrash" films. Mitchell was very pleasant to us and let us hang around whenever he was filming.

Patrick also knew John Pearce, one of the featured players. Pearce had appeared in *The Great Northfield Minnesota Raid* a couple of years earlier. The film was a favorite of Patrick's. Patrick had brought along a 16mm print of the film along with a projector. One evening we set up the projector in Pearce's room, and along with a few six-packs of beer watched it. Well, Pearce, Steve, and Patrick watched the film. I fell asleep, but not before I noticed that in the film Pearce was playing Frank James. The next day, Steve, Patrick, and I were walking near the portable dressing rooms when Lee Marvin passed us while walking to his trailer. "I'm the fastest man in Raintree County!" Patrick blurted out. It was a line of Marvin's from the 1957 movie by the same name. Marvin appeared shocked by the line and turned around to greet Patrick, whose lightning-quick knowledge of Marvin's career impressed the tough-guy actor. Steve and I made our introductions and I quickly pulled out a still from the movie *Prime Cut* and asked for an autograph. Marvin responded with, "I normally don't sign those things, but you guys are different. Come on into my trailer." The actor promptly signed the still as Patrick told Marvin of the television show he was producing. Marvin said he liked the concept but refused an offer to appear on the program (no surprise there). Steve and Patrick spent a good 15 minutes or so chatting with him; I sat there mostly quiet. As we were leaving, Marvin patted Patrick on the shoulder and left a smear of makeup on Patrick's shirt. Marvin apologized and then pulled out a wad of cash from his pocket to pay for the cleaning. "I don't want your money," Patrick told him. I could tell Marvin was impressed. It was the beginning of a friendship between the two that would last until the actor's tragic passing some 13 years later.

The following day we had to clean and leave our motel room because Patrick had some business to handle back in San Francisco. But it was only a few days later that we returned, this time with another guest in tow: The Old Man. The Old Man was on his best behavior. No fights with Steve. No arguing or speaking out of turn. During the evenings, he would join Patrick and Steve across the street from our new motel at a bar. Since I still wasn't of age, I stayed in the room and watched television. The Old Man did teach me an important lesson during the trip. While using a public restroom he yelled out, "Glory-ow-sky! Never use your hand to flush a public toilet, use your foot!" Good lesson learned.

One afternoon while they were shooting a scene at a barbershop between Richard Burton and Cameron Mitchell, Patrick and Lee Marvin decided to play a trick on Mitchell. The scene required Burton to pull down a racist poster tacked to the shop wall and confront Mitchell about it. When Terence Young yelled "Action!" Burton ripped down the poster, but behind it was another one from the film *Gorilla at Large*, a 3-D exploitation movie that had starred Mitchell back in 1954. As fate would have it, Marvin was also in the cast but billed a lowly seventh. Their careers had changed considerably in the intervening 20 years. The poster was courtesy of Patrick. The cast and crew had a big laugh over the prank, as did the startled Mitchell. Terence Young also enjoyed the joke but quickly quieted everyone down and then called for another take.

After the scene was shot properly, Mitchell was kind enough to introduce us to Richard Burton. Burton was sitting alone, relaxing in an empty room in a bus station, waiting for his call to set, sipping on straight vodka from a tumbler filled to the brim with ice, the kind of glass most people would drink water from. After Mitchell told Burton that we were friends, I quickly pulled out my 8x10 still from *Hammersmith is Out*, a film Burton had made a couple of years earlier. Burton read the caption of the still: "Master criminal and nut is out!" He smiled and we all laughed while he signed the picture. Mitchell had started a conversation with the famed Welsh actor and we stuck around to listen. Burton talked in a half-drunk, half-stream-of-consciousness way. His voice was mesmerizing, even hypnotic.

I can remember him sharing a story about his home in Mexico with then-wife Elizabeth Taylor. "I was sitting on the couch reading," he opened. "Elizabeth was in the bedroom napping. I looked out the picture window that overlooked our property and I noticed a line of elephants that were crossing a bridge. 'Elizabeth! There are elephants crossing the Bridge of a Thousand Days!' I shouted. 'Richard,' she replied, 'you simply must stop drinking so much.' I hadn't really been drinking, I just sat there and watched the elephants cross while Elizabeth fell back asleep. The next morning I noticed an article in the newspaper and showed it to Elizabeth—the circus was in town and they had a picture of the elephants walking into town."

Burton was on a roll and kept the stories flowing without interruption. He told us that he had recently held a sword used by Alexander the Great. He could barely lift the huge weapon and was surprised to learn that the famous Greek figure was such a small man. As he continued his stories, the room began to fill up. After a few more tales he noticed that one man was taking notes. "Where are you from?" Burton asked. *The National Enquirer*, the fellow responded. Burton abruptly stood up and left the room. The reporter tried in vain to convince him to stay but to no avail; he was gone, and our time with the famous actor was over.

For a couple of days during filming, Taylor visited the set. Pandemonium ensued. Burton could walk almost anywhere in town without being bothered, but Taylor could barely get out of her chauffeur-driven limousine without being mobbed. I had never seen anything like it. She apparently showed up because there was a rumor going around that Burton had bought a ring for a young girl who worked at a local store. It was the talk of the town, and Taylor wanted to keep an eye on her husband. She would cause calamity anytime she appeared in public. I had no idea just how popular she was until I saw her in Oroville.

Richard Burton and the author on location of *The Klansman*. *(Photo by Steve Monzelli)*

One day, we watched as director Terence Young set up a shot featuring co-star Luciana Paluzzi. It was a simple shot of her opening up a filing cabinet and putting away a couple of folders. And yet, Young was being persistent about getting the shot done correctly. Take after take, Paluzzi was not getting the action to the director's liking. Eventually, he lost his temper, getting down on his knees and grabbing Paluzzi's feet to show the actress exactly where he wanted her to be planted. When they finally had a take he liked, Young called for a break, and we went over to chat with Luciana. We told her how much we had enjoyed her performance in *Thunderball*, and of course, had her pose for photos and sign some stills (we were persistent). She really seemed to enjoy our company, and it was a thrill to meet her after watching the Bond film so many times through the years.

Soon thereafter, Patrick scored a coup, or so we thought. Through his friendship with Cameron Mitchell, he secured an on-camera interview with Burton; not for Patrick's own show, of course, but for a large TV station in Oakland. The station sent a crew to Oroville to film the interview, but on the day of their one-on-one Burton was drunk and uncooperative. The interview was a complete bust. Burton gave one-word answers until Patrick mentioned that Burton had worked with one of his all-time favorite actors. Burton slurred out, "Who was that?" Patrick said "Robert Newton," and Burton changed his attitude instantly. Apparently, he had loved working with Newton, and Burton went on a rant about what a wonderful guy he was. He wouldn't stop telling stories about his late friend. Burton drank continuously through the interview and was now pouring drinks for Patrick. Burton seemed to have an endless supply of Robert Newton stories. When the interview ended, they were both completely wasted, but Patrick was overjoyed that he was able to get Burton to open up a bit. Later, when Patrick showed the footage to the station, they were aghast. They had massive amounts of footage of a drunk Patrick interviewing an even drunker Richard Burton, talking about an actor who almost no one remembers. Nothing that had been shot could be used. The footage never aired.

Lee Marvin between takes while filming *The Klansman*. *(Photo by John Gloske)*

When *The Klansman* finally wrapped, Burton ended up in a clinic to dry out. Lee Marvin gloated, "Who said the Welsh can outdrink an American?" In the finished film, it's quite obvious that Burton was drunk off his ass in more than just a few scenes. Marvin, who seemed to be drinking as much as Burton on the set, comes across just fine. He actually turns in a good performance. Burton doesn't bother to perform; he just stands, or more often sits, and slurs out his lines. Almost no one in the movie has a stellar performance. Paluzzi, who was a delight in person, had her voice obviously dubbed. And Cameron Mitchell did not get the comeback he had hoped for. The movie was a bust; almost worthless really. Burton and Marvin had to sue the producers to get their salaries, and Steve and I never did get those roles as extras. Steve, ever the storyteller, was fond of telling people that he had been directed by Terence Young. "How?" you ask. One day while on set we asked the famed director for a photo, and right before the camera clicked he said to us, "Look directly into the lens." For Steve, that was good enough. "We were directed by Terence Young," he would say. We also did get to see a couple of cinema icons in action, even if it was in the drunken autumn of their years.

This wouldn't be the last time we hung around movie sets. We both figured that we could become actors by simply mingling close to the productions. Steve was much more dedicated to this than I was. He wanted to become an actor, or at the very least a stuntman. With his good looks, charming personality, and fearless attitude, I figured it was not out of the question. Steve had already told so many girls he was an actor, it should just be a short leap to becoming one, right?

In 1974, producer Irwin Allen brought his production of *The Towering Inferno* to San Francisco. Allen had hit the big time a couple of years earlier with *The Poseidon Adventure*. Long before that blockbuster, he had been grinding out sci-fi features and television shows for years. He was now one of the hottest producers in Hollywood and this was to be his follow-up to *Poseidon*. The cast list was like something out of a film fan's favorite dream: Paul Newman, Steve McQueen, William Holden, and Fred Astaire, not to mention O.J. Simpson (again) and many others. Both Steve and I registered at a local casting agency in hopes of getting jobs as extras. We never received a callback, so we took it upon ourselves to be in the film anyway we could; and with Steve around, that meant sneaking past the security guards and into a scene, getting as close to the cameras as possible.

One evening while the company was shooting a night scene at the Bank of America building in downtown S.F., we managed to get ourselves into a crowd of extras, determined to get in the film. They shot late into the night and the company kept us well-fed. Steve carried a bottle of vodka to ward off the chill. The scene called for the building to be lit floor by floor, all the way to the top floor, and the crowd that we were part of was to "ooh" and "ahh" in amazement. It all sounded a little strange to me. How could the building be a surprise to anyone? Didn't the populace of San Francisco see the thing while it was being built? Still, I didn't dare ask any questions; we just did what we were told. Luckily for me, I ended up in the finished film, at least for a second or two. To his chagrin, Steve didn't make the final cut.

If you've been following along, it should come as no surprise that Steve was a huge Steve McQueen fan. During the filming of *The Towering Inferno*, we decided to knock on McQueen's trailer to try and get an autograph. When McQueen answered the door he initially refused Steve's request. He was another Lee Marvin and didn't sign autographs. But after chatting with Steve a bit, he changed his mind. "Aw, come on in, I don't want anyone seeing me doing this," he said. We sat down in his trailer as he wrote on the still, "To Steve, from Steve." McQueen was in full costume and fiddling with his fireman's helmet. He looked at Steve and asked quizzically, "Have you ever seen such a helmet?"

Steve thought for a moment and answered, "Yeah, in a parade."

McQueen let out a laugh and agreed. From that time on they were buddies. McQueen now would always acknowledge Steve by name when he would see him around the set. We weren't being paid, but at least we got to hang around another production and meet our film heroes, at least long enough to get an autograph. The nicest guy on the set was our buddy from *Magnum Force*, Felton Perry, who was also playing a firefighter. Perry loved talking movies and encouraged us to follow our dreams of getting into show business. He even got us some coffee from craft service. He was a great guy.

Around this time, Steve and I, along with Eddie and some of our other film buff friends, were back at the Palace of Fine Arts in San Francisco, where they were holding the annual San Francisco Film Festival. This time it was in tribute to director Francis Ford Coppola. They screened two of his films, *The Rain People* and the musical *Finian's Rainbow* starring Fred Astaire. After the screening, they held a Q&A session with Coppola. I recall the director saying that in the future movies would not be shot on film but digitally. The idea seemed absurd at the time. After attending the tribute to Coppola, we waited outside to meet him. The crowd around the director was thick with fans, but Steve was never shy around anyone; and when he caught a glimpse of the director he blurted out, "Mr. Coppola, you said you're shooting a sequel to *The Godfather*. I'm Italian. I'd like to be in your movie." Surprisingly, Coppola told him that they would be shooting in Lake Tahoe soon and that he should go up there and talk to the casting people. Steve took him at his word and soon after the invitation headed north to Lake Tahoe with Eddie. I passed on the trip. I was working full-time; and besides, I wasn't a big fan of *The Godfather*. I'm embarrassed to say it took years for me to appreciate its brilliance.

Steve and Eddie were gone for about a week. When they returned, Steve claimed he'd been cast as a parking valet. Eddie said he played a waiter in the famous lakeside wedding reception scene. They said they hung out with Robert Duvall, John Cazale, and Troy Donahue, and met Al Pacino long enough to chat for a few minutes and amazingly for Steve to persuade him to do a cameo in the 8mm film Steve was shooting on set. Steve even remembered to have my still autographed by Pacino. Steve hit it off with Cazale, a highly regarded character actor reprising his role as the weak brother Fredo. Steve told him about his desire to be an actor. Cazale advised him to move to New York, study acting, do stage work, then return to California. Good advice, but it meant getting serious about his future and that was too much work for Steve. The more stories they told us, the more I and others began to doubt their validity. As he did produce a paycheck from Paramount Pictures, we knew he did something in the movie.

A couple of months later, Steve and Eddie returned to Lake Tahoe to film additional scenes. Again more stories. This time Steve brought a still camera and returned with photos of himself with Pacino, Duvall, and Donahue. The film took months to shoot and was in post-production for over a year. Stories about the production filled the local newspapers. Steve was lucky enough to attend an early, if not the first, preview of the film held at the Coronet Theater in San Francisco. That night, at work at the Coliseum, he told us what a great film it had turned out to be. He said his role was very prominent and he couldn't wait for us to see it once it was in release. Months again passed before the film was finally out. I sat in a theater with rapt attention, waiting to see my best friend on screen. I sat there and waited and waited; no Steve. He was nowhere to be seen anywhere in the three-hour film. My first thought was, "The lying bastard! He's been bullshitting me for months." However, there had been news reports about Coppola's endless edits and re-edits of the film, so I guessed he'd been cut out. It was a huge disappointment to Steve. He'd been telling everyone for months about his role in the movie. It was a great opening line for picking up girls in bars, and I'm sure it worked often. As an Italian American film buff, to be in *Godfather II* was a huge deal.

Robert Duvall, Troy Donohue and Monzelli between takes on the set of *Godfather II*. *(Photo by Mike Ortiz)*

Before the film's release, Steve wore his participation as a sort of badge of honor. Now it was for nothing. It was just Monzelli bullshit. The film became an instant classic and went on to win many awards. After they saw that he didn't make the final cut, Steve's friends would tell him to shut the fuck up whenever he brought up the film. A few years later, Coppola combined *The Godfather* and *Godfather Part II* for a television special. To my shock and surprise, the additional footage included both Steve and Eddie. Steve could now brag that he was indeed in *Godfather II*. He also had the proof, as he had recorded the entire program on a VHS tape and would gladly show it to anyone who doubted his claim to fame.

In the summer of 1976, Steve and I drove up to Santa Rosa where they were filming a movie we knew nothing about. The film was *Smile* starring Bruce Dern. The director was Michael Ritchie, who had directed Robert Redford in *The Candidate*. I was an extra in that film when I was in high school. It was the first film set I'd ever been on. We figured we were shoo-ins for *Smile* since Steve now had Coppola's *Godfather II* on his resume. Plus, Dern was one of our favorite actors. We wanted to show him our appreciation, so we stopped at a local liquor store and picked up a couple of six-packs. What better gift to give him? When we arrived, the first thing we noticed was the shoot was rather low budget. Not many trucks or crew members. We arrived early in the day and watched them shoot a scene in a small diner. Being a warm and dusty day, we cracked a couple of beers and checked out the action. Dern was busy, so we just kept drinking and watching them work. By the time the crew took a break, we only had a few beers left.

    We approached Dern, introduced ourselves, and offered him what was left of our stash. He thanked us but admitted he did not drink. He did remember meeting us from *The Laughing Policeman* set the previous year; you couldn't have asked for a nicer fellow to talk with. As Steve and I continued to down beers, Dern regaled us with stories about working with various actors and directors. When shooting was about to resume and Dern was called back to the set, we thanked him for his time and he left. We both staggered off and found something else to drink. Later in a local bar, we both agreed on what a great guy Dern was for taking the time to talk with us. Unfortunately, with all the alcohol we consumed, we couldn't really remember anything he said to us. You can only imagine our surprise when months later we watched the finished product in a theater, only to find out it was populated with loads of cute girls appearing as beauty contestants. How did we miss seeing all those girls? Some like Melanie Griffith, Annette O'Toole, and Colleen Camp would soon be major stars.

Bruce Dern and the author between takes on the set of *Smile. (Photo by Steve Monzelli)*

Bruce Dern filming a scene for *Smile (Photo by John Gloske)*

Monzelli and Michael Douglas on location for *The Streets of San Francisco. (Photo by John Gloske)*

Karl Malden and Michael Douglas filming a scene for *The Streets of San Francisco. (Photo by John Gloske)*

From 1972 to '77, the popular show *The Streets of San Francisco* was constantly shooting somewhere in the city. The company even used Patrick's business as base camp for a couple of days. It was a true delight for Patrick. He got to talk with series star Karl Malden about one of his favorite Westerns, *The Hanging Tree*, which Malden appeared in and directed after the original director fell ill. Malden loved talking about old films and Patrick loved to listen. Best of all, he was getting paid for the use of his shop. Co-star Michael Douglas was kind enough to pose for pictures with us. Things went a little differently when we had our encounter with Karl Malden. Steve, as I have mentioned, was always referencing films. He figured everyone would catch all his references, or at least the film buffs would. While walking through the hotel used as a location, we spotted Malden walking toward us. Steve immediately called out to him, "Hi Dad!", a reference to Malden's character in *One-Eyed Jacks*, Sheriff "Dad" Longworth. Malden didn't get the reference; he replied to Steve, "Hello, son." I thought this was pretty cool, but Steve was flummoxed. He thought Malden should have gotten the reference. I told Steve that at least he was pleasant enough to sign a couple of stills for us, and that he should forget about the fact that Malden didn't get his ode to a film he had appeared in over a decade earlier.

The 1970s is remembered as the golden era of film directors. For the first time in film history, directors were as important, if not more important, than some of the lead actors themselves. Robert Altman, Francis Ford Coppola, Martin Scorsese, and Brian De Palma, to name only a few, could bring audiences into theaters as effectively as major onscreen stars. Arguably the biggest name at the time was Sam Peckinpah, who also happened to be the most polarizing. Peckinpah was a hero to us. We didn't really understand the quiet subtleties of his work at the time, but boy did we love the violent action. On one of our earlier trips to Los Angeles, Steve and I went to a taping of *The Merv*

Griffin Show. The guest that night was Jim Backus, who was bemoaning the lack of family-oriented movies coming out of Hollywood. "What films can you bring your family to these days?" Backus asked the audience incredulously.

From the audience, Steve blurted out, "*The Wild Bunch!*"

"*The Wild Bunch*?" Backus responded. Steve and I were the only ones clapping in support of one of our favorite films.

We were elated when we heard the news in the spring of 1975 that Peckinpah would film his new movie, *The Killer Elite*, in San Francisco. It was originally going to be shot in London, but star James Caan didn't want to travel overseas. Since I had previously met Peckinpah, it was now Steve's turn. He had envied our previous encounter and the photos I'd come back with. Once we discovered the hotel that the production company was using, it was easy enough to discover where they were filming. The production office had a bunch of call sheets in a box on the door; the call sheets not only told us the exact location of the filming but also who would be on the set and at what time.

In order to be welcomed on set, we devised a plan. We knew that Sam loved to drink and we knew he loved Mexico, so what better way to be welcomed onto the set than to bring him Mexican beer? We knew of a small Hispanic market in Hayward that sold Tres Equis beer. It was a light version of the popular beer Dos Equis, which was a dark beer at the time. Tres Equis was very difficult to find, but we enjoyed drinking it and knew that the market always seemed to have it in stock. One early morning, Steve and I showed up on the set of *The Killer Elite* with a brown paper shopping bag containing two six-packs of the rare brew. We saw Peckinpah sitting in his director's chair reading something. We approached him, introduced ourselves, and presented him with the gift. He flipped! As fate would have it, Tres Equis was one of his favorite beers. Instantly we were in. We now had an open invitation to visit the set anytime, just so long as we kept Sam supplied with Tres Equis.

Some days and nights The Old Man would join us. The crew thought he was a kick and loved him for the uppers he sold them. They needed them, after all; the days were long and grueling, and the nights just as long and very cold. One day Steve and I, along with The Old Man, drove out to Suisun Bay, north of San Francisco, to watch them film on the reserve fleet of military ships that had been mothballed in the bay since the end of World War II. The area was close to where *Blood Alley* had been filmed some three decades earlier. The company had a small powerboat that would ferry the cast and crew out to the liberty ship that was being used as the location for that day. We climbed aboard the boat, telling the captain that we had something for Sam Peckinpah, and he sped across the bay toward the ship, no questions asked. As we approached, preparing to disembark, the captain received a call on his walkie-talkie. "Who are you bringing aboard?" said the anonymous voice from the speaker. When we told him our names, the production assistant said he had no idea who we were. "Tell Sam I have the Tres Equis beer," Steve told the captain. After a few minutes, the production assistant's voice came back on the radio: "Sam says hurry up and get them on board, he's holding up filming until he gets his beer."

Once on board, we saw co-star Gig Young for the first time. The Old Man didn't recognize him at first. "That was Gig Young? He used to be such a handsome guy," he said. Young had a serious drinking problem; his good looks were a thing of the past. When you watch the film it's obvious that Young is a few beers deep in a few scenes. Three years after completing the film Young shot and killed his young wife, then turned the gun on himself. Sad ending.

Peckinpah deservedly had the reputation of a wild man, but he was always very nice to us. He spoke in a very low voice that was difficult to hear, so you were drawn closer to him, intent on not missing a word of what he was saying. Occasionally, he let me carry his briefcase back to his car at the end of the day, which I considered an honor. One day after filming wrapped, the great director sat down and treated Steve, The Old Man, and me to a reading of an old porno novel he had found. After reading a few pages and laughing out loud more than once, he said, "It just might make a good movie." Peckinpah then put the book in his briefcase. During another visit to the set, we found the company set up for the filming but we couldn't find Peckinpah. The scene was to be shot in an alley in San Francisco's Chinatown. We asked around and someone mentioned he was in a nearby bar, so Steve and I went looking for him. Once inside the bar, it was dark and vacant, with the exception of Peckinpah at one end and the bartender at the other. Peckinpah had not seen us, so Steve asked the bartender, "Give that man another of whatever he's drinking and tell him it's from the Gorch Brothers," a reference to *The Wild Bunch*. It took the Asian bartender a few tries before he was able to correctly pronounce the name "Gorch," but he eventually did as requested. Peckinpah looked shocked upon receiving the drink and then noticed us at the far end of the bar. He motioned for us to come closer then spoke in that distinct voice: "Boys, I'm going to see the Gorch Brothers in L.A. later in the month. I'm going to buy them a drink because they just bought me one." He was one of a kind. As far as we were concerned, he was the perfect picture of a movie director.

"Sam," we would soon refer to him as, seemed to really like us, but he didn't care for The Old Man (he had that effect on people). Patrick from Cinema Treasures visited Sam one night in his hotel room. When Sam answered the door the first thing he asked was, "You didn't bring Monzelli with you, did you? The kid's alright, but I can't take the father." Patrick had some T-shirts made up for the cast and crew. They featured a close-up photo of Peckinpah wearing a bandana with the words, "Your Uncle Sam Wants You" printed below. Peckinpah got a kick out of them, as did we. Years later, Patrick would help with casting Peckinpah's final film, *The Osterman Weekend*. Patrick suggested to Peckinpah to hire Rutger Hauer for the lead, which he did. The producers had wanted to hire Mel Gibson.

The Old Man, Sam Peckinpah and Monzelli on the set of *The Killer Elite. (Photo by John Gloske)*

Monzelli, co-star Bo Hopkins and the author on the set of *The Killer Elite*. *(Photo by Doug Krutilek)*

Newt Arnold, Helmut Dantine, Sam Peckinpah and Bobby Visciglia between takes while filming *The Killer Elite*. *(Photo by Doug Krutilek)*

Sam Peckinpah (seated) and crew are about to film the ending of *The Killer Elite*. *(Photo by John Gloske)*

When the filming of *The Killer Elite* wrapped in San Francisco, the production moved to Los Angeles to film interiors at MGM in Culver City. Sam invited us down to visit the set. During our drive down south, we heard a news report on the radio that Sam had been arrested at LAX. Filming had apparently just wrapped and Sam and a buddy of his were arrested before the flight left the ground, for unruly behavior. We were disappointed that the filming was over, but we were able to walk around the MGM lot without fear that the security guards would find us and toss us out. We peeked into one of the stages and watched Gene Kelly shoot wrap-around scenes for *That's Entertainment II*; not as exciting as watching Sam Peckinpah work, but it was MGM and Kelly had been one of its biggest stars during Hollywood's Golden Age.

A few months later, United Artists held a sneak preview of *The Killer Elite* at Northpoint Cinema in San Francisco. Steve and I could hardly wait for the event. Surely, we thought, this would be yet another classic Peckinpah film. When the day arrived, we were among the first in line for the screening. While waiting in the lobby we watched for cast and crew members to show up. We saw Sam, who seemed happy to see us, but not many others connected with the film. A woman approached Steve and smiled at him and gushed, "Mr. Mineo, I just love your work."

"I'm not Sal Mineo!" Steve snapped. He would occasionally be mistaken for the actor, and rightfully so; they could have been brothers. But since Mineo was gay, the comparison bothered Steve.

Once inside the theater, we sat in giddy anticipation of the film beginning. As the film was unspooled, it didn't take us long to realize the movie was a bomb. Some of the scenes looked like they were improvised; and worse yet, improvised by actors who were drunk or perhaps high. The film was unlike any Peckinpah film that preceded it—it was painfully dull. Sam had included a scene with Bo Hopkins alive and well at the conclusion of the film, even though his character had been killed earlier in the movie. This scene was re-cut for the general release version. As we left the screening we were both disappointed that the film had turned out so poorly. I sometimes wonder if, between The Old Man's pills and our Tres Equis beer, we were in some small way responsible for the low quality of the movie. Frank Capra had once said, "There are no rules in filmmaking, only sins, and the cardinal sin in filmmaking is dullness." Every few years or so I pull out my DVD (now Blu-ray) copy of *The Killer Elite* and watch it, hoping I can see something I had previously missed, realizing that perhaps it really is a good film. No such luck. Sam, you made a dull film.

An offer of free booze played an important part in our meeting another celebrity the following year. In this instance, it was Oliver Reed. Director Dan Curtis, who was well-known for his cult television soap opera *Dark Shadows*, was prepping his new horror film. Curtis chose the Dunsmuir House in Oakland for the location of his feature film *Burnt Offerings*. The stellar cast included Bette Davis, Burgess Meredith, Karen Black, Eileen Heckart, and making his debut in an American film, English actor Reed. Reed had a well-earned reputation for being not only a very intense actor but also a world-class hellraiser. He had started his career in Hammer horror films such as *Curse of the Werewolf* before graduating to classier English films like *Women in Love* and *The Devils*. As fate would have it, Steve lived only a few miles from the Dunsmuir House. On one of the first days of filming, Steve and I showed up on the set, watching the crew get ready for a shot, when we noticed Reed sitting alone, apart from the rest of the cast. His temper was legendary—as were his pub fights back in England—but we were not worried. We thought we had just the thing to make him happy.

We approached the actor, stuck out our hands to shake his, and I spoke up and said, "Hello Mr. Reed. We just wanted to say welcome to the United States, and we have a gift for you." We presented him with a brown paper bag containing a fifth of Wild Turkey. "Here is a bottle of American whisky for you," we continued. "We wanted you to know that you have many fans in the United States." Reed pulled the bottle out of the sack and a wide smile appeared across his face, unlike any I had ever seen him flash on screen. He thanked us profusely and asked us our names, as he quickly unscrewed the bottle and took a long swig. We asked him if we could take some photos together and he happily obliged. From that moment on, we were in.

The production company stayed at a hotel in nearby Berkeley. Since arriving there, there had been an ongoing problem between Reed and his female co-star Bette Davis. It seemed that Reed would get drunk at the hotel bar late at night and then use the room service carts as surfboards. He would ride the carts up and down the hallway, yelling as he went. Davis was livid. When word of her displeasure got back to Reed, he apologized and ended his nightly ritual. It's a shame we didn't bother to mention the hotel's fire escape system to Reed. Years earlier, Steve and I, along with various high school friends, would frequently go to the hotel, take the elevator to the top floor, walk to the end of the long hallway, open up the fire escape door (which contained an enclosed spiral-type slide), then in total darkness jump into the slide and ride it down 10 floors to the ground. You had to be very quiet not to get caught, but it was a real thrill. Reed would have loved it.

Steve and I saw Reed in the bar and on the set frequently. We never did experience any of his legendary bad behavior. It was always, "Hello boys! How are you?" every time he saw us. I guess we just got off on the right foot. We did approach Bette Davis just once, in the hotel lobby. I requested an autograph, as did Steve. Her temper was also something of legend and we didn't know what to expect. She responded, "Certainly." What a surprise. She asked our names and when she finished with the autograph told us, "Thank you for asking. Have a nice day." *Burnt Offerings* would turn into a minor cult film, slowly paced but tension-filled and extremely creepy. Oliver Reed is excellent, playing his character very low key, which was a drastic change from some of his better-known films. Stephen King credits *Burnt Offerings* with influencing his writing of the novel *The Shining*.

Oliver Reed shows off his gift from Monzelli and the author between takes during the filming of *Burnt Offerings*. *(Photo by John Gloske)*

Having missed our chance to meet Hitchcock a few years earlier in Los Angeles, we were thrilled to learn that the iconic director would be shooting his latest movie in San Francisco. The film was originally titled *Deceit* and later changed to *Family Plot*. We found the production shooting at Grace Cathedral Episcopal Church on Nob Hill. The star of the film was Bruce Dern, who we now considered our buddy, having met him on two other film shoots and once at the Coliseum when he was watching a Warriors basketball game. We re-introduced ourselves and he seemed genuinely happy to see us. We thanked him for killing off John Wayne's character in *The Cowboys*, a film released a few years earlier that Patrick had recently screened for us in his basement theater. Not many actors can lay claim to having dusted the Duke on screen. He laughed and told us, "The hippies loved that I killed Wayne in that movie, but when I'm in the South I have to hide my face." We sat with him in a pew, talking movies until he was needed for a scene. We always made it a point to be informed about anyone we would meet, so we could actually converse with them and not come off sounding like just another fan; being sober this time helped, too. Nothing pleases an actor or director more than telling them you enjoyed some really obscure film they did that had slipped through the cracks, and Dern had plenty of those in his filmography.

The *Family Plot* set was rather unusual. Everyone, including the crew, was dressed in a suit and tie, and this wasn't just the people working in the church. When I noticed that Hitchcock was not too busy, I slipped over to his chair and pulled out my 8x10 that I had been trying to get him to sign for years. I caught his attention and spoke up. "Mr. Hitchcock, my name is John. Would you autograph this for me?" I handed him the still and a pen.

"Certainly, John, and thank you," he replied. He signed the still, handed it back, and I slipped away. Mission accomplished, finally.

Family Plot turned out to be the final film directed by Hitchcock. It wasn't up there with his classics, but it was certainly a nice, lighthearted film, well-made and enjoyable.

Bruce Dern during the filming of Alfred Hitchcock's final film *Family Plot. (Photo by John Gloske)*

Steve would persist in finding work in movies. If he wasn't hired on as a non-union extra, he would sneak into a crowd scene. It never mattered if he was paid or not; he just wanted to be on the big screen. Steve, along with Eddie, appeared for a few seconds in *More American Graffiti*, the little-known sequel to the hit film, as well as in *Freebie and the Bean*; and he also claimed to be in the opening credits for the TV show *The Dain Curse*, but as I never saw the show I can't substantiate his claim. Other sets we visited during this period included *Street People*, where we got to meet Roger Moore (who had replaced Sean Connery in the James Bond series a few years earlier); and *Skyjacked*, filmed at the Oakland Airport which was standing in for an airport in Anchorage, Alaska. The star of the film, Charlton Heston, was nice enough to sign some stills from *The Planet of the Apes*, along with a one-sheet poster to *The Omega Man*. However, he didn't seem impressed when I told him I could recite the dialog from one of Cornelius's speeches in *Beneath the Planet of the Apes*. Other film sets we checked out were *Time After Time* starring cult actor Malcolm McDowell, and *Mr. Billion*, a movie with a strong cast of character actors, including Jackie Gleason, Slim Pickens, Chill Willis, William Redfield, and Dick Miller. I don't think the film was ever released, at least not in the Bay Area. Film production in San Francisco seemed nonstop during this time.

Roger Moore and Monzelli on location for *Street People*. *(Photo by John Gloske)*

Late in 1976, Steve attended a lecture at UC Berkeley given by Martin Scorsese. He wanted to see if lightning could strike twice. After the talk he approached the famed director, told him he was also Italian, and handed him a headshot of himself with contact information on the back. "I'm available to work anytime if you need me," he told the director. Scorsese never called, which was unfortunate. Steve would have fit in just fine in the film Scorsese was prepping at the time, *New York, New York*. With his on-camera work, it wasn't a far stretch for Steve to now introduce himself as an actor when he met people in bars or on the street. If he wanted to be more vaguer, he would simply say, "I'm in the movie business." That line was especially important for him when he was meeting women. Women, at least the ones he would meet, seemed to be more impressed if he introduced himself as an actor than just a third baseman.

THE BIG HEAT

Palo's Place was a mid-scale restaurant/bar, an extremely popular place during the mid-1970s, located at the east end of Fisherman's Wharf, one of San Francisco's most popular tourist attractions. The streets around Palo's brimmed with buskers trying to make a buck from the hordes of out-of-towners who visited. Steve loved Palo's for two reasons. First and most important, it was a hangout for female tourists looking for a good time. Steve could assume any identity he wanted to and, more often than not, get laid. And since the women were only in town for a few days, there was never a question about starting a relationship. The second reason Steve loved Palo's was that after the bar closed, the owners would put on poker games and those who were chosen to stay could keep ordering liquor. Steve was always among the chosen ones. The staff enjoyed his sense of humor and his money. The fact that the owners were Italian helped some too.

After one particularly long night of drinking, Steve ended up in the parking lot of Palo's, locked in a torrid embrace with a woman he'd met earlier at the bar. She wanted to go down on him as he leaned against a parked car, which was fine with Steve; but just before she did, Steve slid his hand down the front of her pants and to his shock grabbed a dick. He immediately lost his temper, going berserk and beating the hell out of this poor transgendered person. Someone from Palo's tried pulling Steve off, but he had flipped the switch to full psycho, firing punch after punch into the person. Finally, with the help of another patron, they were able to pull Steve away. Shortly after, the sound of police sirens began to fill the air. Hearing the approaching squad cars,

Steve came to his senses and jumped in a nearby taxi cab and took off, disappearing into the early morning fog.

The next day in my apartment Steve explained to me what had happened. He regretted losing his temper but he admitted he just flipped out. He showed me his scarred hands, evidence of the horrible beating he had given out. I joked with him that subconsciously he really knew the woman was a guy, and that he was, in fact, looking for a dick. He was not amused. Seeing him get so upset about the joke was strange since normally nothing was out of bounds when it came to Steve's humor. After the parking lot incident, it would be weeks before he would show his face at Palo's Place again.

By the late 1970s, the punk music phenomenon had hit the Bay Area by storm. North Beach, an old Italian immigrant enclave with wonderful restaurants and colorful streets, was now a rather sleazy area featuring live nude sex shows in the numerous bars and nightclubs that dotted Broadway and Columbus. One night Steve was watching a band perform in a particularly hot and crowded club. The music was overpowering and you had to scream to be heard by the cocktail waitresses. Steve had been drinking beer the entire show and finally decided to ask somebody who was playing. "The Dead Kennedys," they told him. The name infuriated him. The more he thought about a music group named after the two assassinated Kennedy brothers, the angrier he grew. At one point he became so enraged he threw a beer bottle at the head of the lead singer and connected. That quickly set off a brawl that poured into the street. One of the bouncers realized that it was Steve who had started the ordeal. When the burly security guard pushed his way through the crowd and got close enough to Steve, he shot him directly in the face with mace. The hit was brutal—Steve dropped to his knees, screaming, unable to see anything. Well, that only escalated things. The club quickly erupted into a full-scale riot, people fighting all around him. Steve, even with his eyes stinging and blurry, knew the place well enough to find his way outside. He could hear the wail of the police sirens fast approaching. Once outside, he started to get his vision back, at least enough to run the few blocks to his car and drive home.

Steve escaped the cops that night, but he hadn't learned his lesson to stay out of North Beach. A few weeks later he was back, downing shots of Stoli and having no luck trying to pick up one of the many girls in another crowded nightclub. He left for greener pastures, specifically Union Street. It was more upscale, which meant the drinks were costlier, but it was worth a try. Behind the wheel of his shiny white '67 Mustang Fastback (the same type used by Steve McQueen in *Bullitt*), Steve gunned the engine and sped wildly down the darkened streets, lit only by neon signs; his skill behind the wheel would have impressed McQueen, I'm sure of it. But his stunt driving didn't impress the San Francisco Police Department. Within minutes they were right on his tail with their red lights blazing and sirens screaming. Steve knew he was too drunk to explain his way out of this one, so he jammed his foot on the gas and decided to try and outrun San Francisco's finest. He quickly made a sharp turn up a steep hill and floored the gas pedal again. Steve didn't realize what the cops surely did: it was a dead-end street with pylons at the top. The pylons didn't bother Steve. To evade the police he drove on the sidewalk and between the pylons, missing them by mere inches. Unfortunately, the cops had radioed for backup, and another patrol car was waiting for Steve as he emerged from the sidewalk. As they were handcuffing him, one of the officers admitted to being impressed by Steve's driving. Steve appreciated the compliment. He spent most of the next day in jail with the satisfaction that at least one officer in the SFPD thought his skills behind the wheel were rather spectacular.

By the end of 1978, I was getting tired of the Bay Area, so I talked Steve into moving to Lake Tahoe. "Hell, we've spent so much time there, why not just move there?" I told him. "We can gamble and drink around the clock, and just think of the women we could have with all our winnings." Steve thought it was a good idea, too. We checked into getting jobs at the casinos over the phone but they told us we would have to move there before they would consider us. That was fine with us. We had enough money from the recent football season (the Raiders had won the Super Bowl) to last a few months, even if we didn't find jobs immediately. The plan was set in motion.

Eventually, I moved, but Steve stayed put. He just couldn't conceive of leaving San Francisco. He loved the city and it loved him back. Plus, he couldn't stomach the thought of saying goodbye to his favorite bars, and the women in those bars. I remained in Lake Tahoe for about six months, then moved back, broke and despondent. On my first night back in the Bay Area I was again selling beer at the Oakland Coliseum. It was a strange feeling. Everything and everybody was the same. The conversations were the same. The arguments were the same. I couldn't stand it. I quit after one night. As I was about to leave the building I noticed a long line of vendors snaking out of the men's restroom. "Why the long line?" I asked. Turns out a drunk woman was giving free blowjobs in one of the stalls. I kept walking and thought, "Well, some things have changed."

Later that night at Sam's Hof Brau, Steve told me, "John, get out of here. You deserve better. If you don't get out now you'll wind up like these guys." He pointed out the other beer vendors who were drunk and trying desperately to pick up the equally drunk women. I took his sage advice. Within a few months, I moved to Los Angeles. Meanwhile, Cinema Treasures had become Steve's second home, and Patrick became his number one drinking buddy. Patrick's knowledge of film history was beyond even Steve's. Patrick knew of the most obscure films and actors. He was lightning-quick with knowledge of B-films, from the 1930s through '50s to the Cinerama epics of the '60s, all Westerns, all foreign films, and virtually everything in between. He was truly amazing. With their mutual love of cinema and liquor, it was a friendship made in heaven.

One night Steve and Patrick were at Patrick's home in San Francisco, downing shots of vodka in the kitchen. "Let's go hit some bars," Steve suggested. Patrick agreed. It was always best to get a buzz first at the house and then move on to the bars. It was too expensive to just start drinking at the bar. Patrick offered to drive. Steve hadn't finished his drink so he took it along for the ride. ("Never waste liquor," Steve was fond of saying.) Patrick was driving his pickup truck through the heavy downtown San Francisco traffic when some bozo in a car behind them started honking his horn at Patrick, who was only trying to inch his way through the sea of stagnant vehicles. Steve leaned out of the window, extended his middle finger, and shouted, "Fuck you!"

The angered driver pulled alongside and yelled back at Steve, "FUCKING FARMER!" He then sped up and cut ahead of the two.

Steve was perplexed. *I've been called many things in my life, but never a farmer*, he thought. The more he thought about it, the more pissed he became. "Speed up and catch that asshole," he told Patrick. When they were close enough, Steve finished the remaining vodka in his glass and threw the glass at the offending driver's car. It was a direct hit. Broken glass flew everywhere. The other car sped off in a flash hoping to avoid further confrontation.

Patrick yelled at Steve, "That was one of my wife's favorite glasses!"

Steve responded calmly, "Don't worry, I'll make it up to her."

The duo found a watering hole downtown to continue the evening's drinking. Even after the glass-throwing episode, Steve's frustration over the run-in with the driver was high. "He called me a farmer! Why in the *hell* would he call me a farmer?" Patrick tried to ignore the rants, but the more Steve drank the more perplexed he became. "He called me a FARMER!" Steve was now shouting for all to hear. Finally, Patrick couldn't take it any longer. He grabbed Steve and told him to follow him to his truck. Once outside, standing next to his vehicle, he pointed out the license plate—"Nebraska." Patrick had registered the truck out of state. Now that Steve finally understood the farmer reference, the two walked back into the bar. Once inside, a smiling Steve shouted out proudly for all to hear, "Maybe they thought we were blood farmers!", a reference to the film *Invasion of the Blood Farmers.*

That evening Steve and Patrick wound up back at Patrick's house. Steve crashed on the couch and left early the next morning. A few hours later, Patrick's wife woke up and made her way to the kitchen to make coffee. She yelled at Patrick to come quickly. "What are all these steak knives doing in the sink?" she asked.

Patrick explained, "Steve broke one of your glasses and that's his way of making it up to you. He stole a bunch of knives from a restaurant bar we were at."

The time in the pickup wasn't the only name-calling incident. Another time, Steve and Patrick were walking around Ghirardelli Square in San Francisco. They had been drinking all day and were searching for a new bar to hang out in. As they walked through the courtyard of the famed tourist spot, Steve nearly ran into a woman who was walking with her daughter. The young girl was eating a large cookie. Steve, who was well on his way to being drunk, stopped before colliding with the woman, eyed the young daughter, and then in a good-natured way raised his arms and growled, "I am the cookie monster!"

The mother snapped back, "Don't talk to my daughter! You're nothing but filth!"

At first, Steve was perplexed, then amused. The mother hurried her daughter away, and then Steve turned and flashed that Monzelli smile and said to Patrick, "I like that name. You can call me Filth if you want. It can be my nickname." Steve considered getting a personalized license plate with the word FILTH on it. As he explained to Patrick, "It's not a swear word. They'll have to give it to me!" The idea was later dropped.

Mia, Patrick's wife, was largely understanding of Steve's eccentric personality. She had learned early on to expect—and accept—his unusual behavior. One morning around 5 a.m. there was a loud banging at Patrick and Mia's back door. Patrick went downstairs to investigate and when he looked out there was Steve, wearing only a shirt and socks. "What in the fuck are you doing here? Where are your clothes?" Patrick inquired. Steve explained that he had met a couple of women in a bar hours earlier and, after several drinks, the three had decided to go somewhere to fuck. They piled into one of the women's cars and wound up at a beach somewhere near the avenues. They found a secluded spot on the fog-bound beach with its heavy crashing waves. Steve took on the first woman. After he came, the second woman demanded that he fuck her as well. He obliged and fucked her until he came again. Then the first woman wanted him to do her a second time. "You'll have to give me a little time, I can't do it again so quickly," Steve told her. With that, both women became angry and began yelling at him for not being able to get it up. The argument continued until the first woman gave him the finger and yelled, "Fuck you!" In an instant, they were both back in their car speeding away down the coast highway, quickly disappearing into the night with much of Steve's clothes with them. It was a very long and cold walk to Patrick's house, especially without shoes, but it was the only place a nearly naked Steve could go.

Steve and Patrick had been to the same beach a few months earlier. Patrick, his cousin Edwin, and Steve had been out of town on a three-day bender. Patrick was driving along the coast, heading home, when Steve yelled out, "Pull the car over!" Patrick told Steve to shut up, but Steve yelled out louder, "Pull the fucking car over!" Patrick did as requested.

Once the car came to a stop along the side of the road, Patrick turned to Steve and asked in wonderment, "Why did you want me to pull over?"

Steve, who was feeling the full effects of three days of hard drinking, replied, "I have a heat on, I've got to swim the heat off." With that, Steve bolted out of the car, stripped to his shorts, and sprinted into the ocean.

Edwin went berserk. "He'll fucking drown," he exclaimed. "No one swims here, and there's sharks out there." The two looked on in disbelief as Steve dove into the surf and disappeared into the raging waves. They were correct—no one swims in that part of the ocean—and no one except for them was even on the beach. They scanned the menacing surf, but neither of them could spot Steve. They paced the sand yelling out for Steve for over 20 minutes, to no avail; they were convinced that Steve had drowned. Patrick even for a moment thought that maybe Steve wanted to go out like Norman Maine in *A Star is Born*.

Suddenly, Steve emerged from the swirling sea, gasping for breath and shaking from the freezing water. He looked at his two friends and stated simply, "It worked. I swam the heat off. Let's go home." They did just that.

Vending at the Coliseum and Candlestick Park paid well, but Steve's lifestyle was getting expensive. His increasing popularity at the local bars meant that he inevitably ended up paying for not only his drinks, but the drinks of friends, old and new. And although the hookers he liked were still cheap (relatively speaking), they wanted to get paid upfront—no credit. When he would run up a large tab at a bar he couldn't pay, he would simply stay away for a few weeks, until the proprietors started making threats. Steve was constantly in need of cash and fast; cash would rarely come fast. Besides collecting movie posters and 16mm films, Steve still had his enormous collection of comic books, all sealed in plastic. It was now time to start selling off his comic book collection a few pieces at a time.

He discovered a store on Fisherman's Wharf that gladly bought whatever he brought in. It hurt him to do this—he was a collector after all—but he needed the money. Bit by bit, his collection dwindled, but he made a load of money from it. Yes, it was mostly drank, gambled, and whored away, but it did keep him supplied with cash for months. The extra money also came in handy when Steve was audited by the IRS. You see, Steve had been claiming his father as a dependent on his personal income tax for years. The Old Man had been on disability, so the idea wasn't much of a stretch. The IRS caught on and didn't buy the deduction, and demanded the money back. They went so far as to assign a keeper to Steve. The keeper would show up at the Coliseum after the games and wait for Steve to check out. Immediately upon receiving his cash commission for the evening, Steve had to hand over a big stack to the keeper. Fortunately, the keeper didn't know about the comic book income.

A lesson I learned early on from Steve was that if you wanted something, anything, go for it. Be bold and do it. It's an important lesson. Steve was fearless (or at least he appeared that way), and it was a trait I always admired in him. He hated the word "don't" or "can't." To drive the point home, one night in San Francisco Patrick and Steve were in a bar, downing shots of vodka. There was a large mirror above the bar and Steve noticed that baseball legend Joe DiMaggio was sitting alone and drinking only a few feet away. "I'm going to say hello to Joltin' Joe," he told Patrick.

Patrick looked horrified and responded in a hushed tone, "No, never talk to DiMaggio. Everyone knows his reputation. He's a real jerk. You always leave him alone. Don't even think about it."

Steve ignored Patrick's advice and got out of his chair, approaching the baseball icon. DiMaggio noticed Steve standing before him and looked up from his drink, glaring hard at him. Always fearless, Steve calmly stated, "Hi Mr. DiMaggio, my name is Steve Monzelli. My uncle Paul Monzelli played in the Pacific Coast League with you." DiMaggio thought for a moment (everyone thought he was going to tell Steve to get the hell away from him), and responded with, "Yes he did. He was a fine player. I see the family resemblance. Sit down and I'll buy you a drink."

Steve called Patrick over and the two spent the rest of the evening drinking on DiMaggio's dime and talking about the long-gone days of the Pacific Coast League. Steve's Uncle Paul was indeed a well-respected player in his day, but the word was that he couldn't hold his liquor and that it eventually got the best of him. He never achieved the star player status that most people thought he should have.

On another night before Steve and Patrick headed out for an evening of drinking, they stopped at the office of a friend of Patrick's. This friend was doing post-production work on a feature he had just directed. They noticed an old man sleeping on the floor in the corner of the office. The man turned out to be none other than noted film director Nicholas Ray. Long past his 1950s prime, Ray awoke, shook his head, and noticed Steve and Patrick. Introductions were made, and Steve asked Ray if he wanted to join them at a bar down the street.

"I'm broke," the old director informed them.

Steve smiled and responded with, "Don't worry about it."

The trio walked down the street in North Beach and entered a popular bar called Tosca. Once inside, Steve perused the clientele and didn't like what he saw. High-class wannabes bothered him. "I'm not drinking with Mephistos!" he shouted for all to hear, referencing the film *Mephisto Waltz*, a reference only Patrick was likely to understand. "I know a better place," he continued. "Let's get the hell out of here." The three left and wound up at one of Steve's favorite bars, where the drinks were cheap and the patrons looked like exiles from a Fellini movie. Ray didn't know what to make of the pair of film buffs, but after a couple of drinks, he warmed up to them and delighted them with endless stories of Old Hollywood. Ray admitted he had made a fortune working at RKO back in Hollywood's golden age. Howard Hughes had owned the studio at the time, and his slate of films turned out to be mostly clunkers. Hughes had Ray re-shoot and re-edit the troubled productions so they could be profitably released. Ray worked uncredited on numerous films, and with his directorial skills was occasionally able to turn their fate around. Ray regaled the duo with stories of working with James Dean and Natalie Wood on *Rebel Without a Cause*. Steve and Patrick were in movie buff paradise. Ray admitted drinking all his money away. He was broke and truly grateful for the free drinks they bought for him. Steve and Patrick decided they were well worth it.

Steve's charm allowed him to get away with all types of antisocial behavior. His was not some phony, concocted made-up charm, but the kind that only comes naturally. He knew that he had it, and he certainly knew how to use it. He charmed countless women out of their clothes and into his bed, car, or just wherever. He seemed to be able to charm just about anyone. Case in point, one night as he walked through an upscale area of San Francisco on his way to a girlfriend's apartment, he happened to pass by the Russian embassy. This was during the early Eighties when the Cold War was still in full swing. He noticed a limousine at the front entrance that was surrounded by lights and news cameras. He got closer and noticed that they were interviewing a visiting Russian dignitary.

Steve stood by and watched until the news crews finished. When he saw his chance he went right up to the Communist bigwig and said, "Welcome to San Francisco, sir. I just wanted you to know that most Americans really love Russians." The fellow's face lit up and he thanked Steve for the greeting. But Steve went on. "I also want you to know that I love Russian vodka. As a sign of our mutual friendship, I would gladly accept a bottle." Amazingly, the dignitary turned to an aide and yelled a command in Russian. The aide disappeared into the embassy only to reemerge a few moments later with a bottle of Stolichnaya. Steve shook the dignitary's hand and thanked him profusely. Now well-supplied for a night of fun, he continued the walk to the apartment. Steve showed the bottle to his girlfriend at the time, Patti. It had a blue label, all in Russian, not the imported red label that we see domestically. This was the real Russian vodka, the good stuff they save for themselves. Steve opened the bottle and poured out shots for them both. Since she had known Steve for some time at that point, she was impressed but not necessarily surprised.

Since I was now living in Los Angeles, I didn't see much of Steve during the early 1980s. We would talk on the phone probably once a week; and I noticed that when we did, he was drunk more often than not. He called one night, very late, drunk and upset. He had just seen the newest Bond film, *For Your Eyes Only*. He enjoyed the film but was incensed that John Barry was not hired to compose the musical score, as he had on almost all the previous Bond films. "Why the fuck didn't they hire him? It would have been a great film!" Steve lamented. I agreed, but what else could I say about it? Steve went on and on; he wouldn't let the topic change. He took it as a personal affront that Barry was not hired. "Steve, let it go, maybe he'll do the next film," I told him, just wanting to change the subject. Something like this could piss him off for weeks. As he kept repeating the same rants over and over again, I began to realize that the booze now controlled Steve and not the other way around.

On occasion, I would drive the 350 miles north to the Bay Area for a visit. Since Steve was almost never home, I would have to drive the streets of San Francisco checking in at his favorite bars just to find him. It was much easier than it sounds, since everyone in the bars seemed to know Steve, so someone always knew where he was. On one such visit, I found him in a seedy nightclub downtown. He was sitting at the bar, well on his way to a good drunk, and keeping the bartender entertained with stories and dirty jokes. After we talked for a bit, I told him we should go out and get something to eat. He explained to me in all seriousness, "John, I don't really need to eat food anymore. I just drink vodka." With typical Steve logic, he went on to explain, "People die from drinking bad booze. I only drink the good stuff, Stolichnaya. It supplies me with all the nutrients I need. I've been off food for some time now. I really don't miss it." He did look leaner than the last time I saw him, but I didn't want to compliment him on his unusual weight-loss regime. There was really no need to try to talk him out of his lifestyle. I knew he wouldn't listen, so I never bothered. Eddie once asked me to talk Steve into sobriety, but I refused. What could I tell him that he didn't already know?

Later that night we were back at his apartment in Oakland. It was surprisingly clean and neatly arranged. He had his 16mm projector set up and ready to go so that he could watch a movie from his collection whenever he got home. It was a nightly ritual. Videotapes had just arrived on the market and his collection of VHS tapes was starting to grow, but it was 16mm film that he loved the most. Steve would spend most of his money on booze, but what little was leftover would still go for movie memorabilia, most often purchased from Patrick at Cinema Treasures. The walls of his apartment were lined with classic movie posters. His centerpiece was *Casablanca*. He had purchased it for less than $5 back in high school, and even back then it was a collector's item. He didn't mind selling off his comics; but his movie poster collection, that was another story.

Steve's curiosity streak caused problems on more than one occasion. Steve and Patrick were barhopping once around Market Street in downtown San Francisco, and were both well drunk by the time they wandered over to an open manhole. Steve peered down the hole but could not see the workers, only the faint light that came from deep inside the sewer system. "I've always wanted to see what the inside of a sewer looked like," Steve told Patrick. His curiosity was no doubt fueled by watching *The Third Man* too many times. As Patrick watched in amazement, Steve climbed down the ladder and into the bowels of the city. Steve disappeared from view, but Patrick heard the following conversation echoing out of the sewer system:

"*Who* the *fuck* are you?"

"I just wanted to see what's going on down here!"

"Get the fuck out of here!"

"I'm just looking!"

"Get the fuck out now!"

Patrick watched as Steve scampered up the temporary ladder and back up onto the street. Once aboveground, Steve pulled the ladder out of the hole and then slid the manhole cover back into place. Patrick was stunned as they heard muffled screams from below. "What the fuck did you do? Come back, you asshole!" Undeterred, Patrick and Steve scampered down the street and found another bar, as the drunken buzz they both shared earlier started to wear off.

Later that night at last call, Patrick asked Steve if he wanted to crash at his place. Patrick hoped to avoid the 30-minute drive across the Bay Bridge to Oakland. "My girlfriend Toni lives right down the street," Steve replied. "Let's walk over to her house." Once at the apartment building, Steve tried the buzzer. No answer. "Let's go around to the alley," he told his buddy. Once in the alley, Steve did his best Stanley Kowalski impression. "Toni! Toooooni!" he screamed … and he did really have to yell at the top of his lungs, as she lived on the fourth floor. No response. "Toni! Toni!" he screamed again.

A Chinese woman on the third floor opened her window and yelled, "You go away! It's two o'clock in the morning! You drunk!" She was correct on both accounts. Steve yelled again, only this time much louder. The woman disappeared from the window and returned in a few moments with a bucket of water that she promptly dumped on Steve. Steve took the hit and spent the next few hours on Patrick's couch sobering up and drying off.

Patrick did not like drinking in Oakland. He found the city just too rough. It was known at the time as the murder capital of the nation. Against his better judgment, one Saturday afternoon Patrick and Steve were cruising the streets of downtown Oakland and Steve wanted a drink. Patrick refused the request. The bars they passed looked too intimidating. Exasperated, Steve yelled out, "Just pull over at the bar on the next corner. I'll go in myself, only for a minute." Patrick did as Steve requested. The bar door was open and Patrick watched from the car as Steve entered. As Steve promised, one minute later he exited running at full speed, carrying a bar stool. He quickly opened the back door of the car, tossed the stool inside, and yelled to Patrick, "Step on it, they're after us!" Steve jumped in the passenger seat and the duo hit the road.

Patrick yelled at Steve, "You stole a barstool? Why in the hell did you do that?"

Steve replied, "Let's head to my apartment and have a drink."

Upon entering his apartment, Steve placed the barstool next to an identical one that he had stolen from the same bar the previous week. "Now we can drink at my bar!" he exclaimed. With matching barstools his own private bar was complete. After a couple of drinks, Patrick wanted to get back to the city. "Not yet!" Steve told his buddy, "I have to iron my clothes first." Steve always wore well-pressed clothes. As Steve ate up important barhopping time with his ironing, Patrick became incensed and told him, "Steve, you're ironing your clothes every time I'm here. Why don't you get a job at a dry cleaner?" Steve smiled, doing his Burt Reynolds laugh, and kept on ironing.

In fall 1984 it was announced with great fanfare that the next James Bond film, *A View To A Kill,* would be partially filmed in San Francisco and its surrounding enclaves. For a lifelong James Bond fan like Steve, it was a dream come true. Patrick had no desire to be an actor or even an extra, so it was Steve and Eddie who showed up during the filming at City Hall. This wasn't *Godfather II*; no one on the production wanted to pay them for being extras, as all the casting had already been completed. On the set, Steve did spot Albert R. Broccoli, famed Bond producer. Steve promptly walked over to him, shook his hand, and thanked him for producing so many great 007 films. Broccoli was very pleasant, but he was hurried off by an assistant before Steve could ask for a role; or perhaps, more importantly, ask why John Barry didn't score *For Your Eyes Only*. As he had done so many times before, Steve snuck into a crowd scene with Eddie. No one caught on, and they stayed with the crowd until the scene was completed. When the film was finally released, Steve swore he was in it. I have seen the film a couple of times and never spotted him, but Eddie does appear quite prominently in one scene.

Occasionally Steve would come down and visit me in LA. I picked him up from LAX one night and we promptly headed for a nightclub in Universal City. When we left the club Steve was drunk off his ass. Instead of holding on to the handrail while walking down the steps to the parking lot, he decided to sit on the rail and slide down to the bottom. Slide he did, very rapidly, until he began to lose his balance and spin. The loud crack I heard was Steve's head hitting the concrete stairs. He lay motionless at the bottom of the stairs for what seemed like an eternity. I helped him up and into the car, where he sat down without a word and was out again in an instant. Fifteen minutes later I was almost back at my apartment when he finally came to. The first words out of his mouth were, "Shit, feel the bump on my head." I did and it was enormous. The next words were, "I don't know about you, but I'd like to find an after-hours club." Since I had to get up at 7 AM the next morning the idea didn't really appeal to me. But Steve was serious, so I dropped him off—head wound and all—at Cahoots, a popular club about five blocks from my apartment. He borrowed some money from me and walked into the club. I drove home to sleep.

The next morning I awoke to find no Steve. He had a key, so I locked the door and went to work. When I arrived home that evening, still no Steve. He didn't arrive until almost midnight. It turned out that he had met a woman in the club. After the place closed she tried to drive him to my building, but Steve was too drunk to give her directions. She drove him back to her apartment for a couple more drinks, and then to the bed for some drunk sex. He spent that night with her, as well as the rest of the following day. When they got tired of fucking they went looking for my building again. She spent that evening cruising the streets of Glendale until Steve could finally find it.

A couple of days later I had a meeting at Paramount Studios in Hollywood. I received permission from studio operations to bring Steve along and give him a tour before my appointment. It was very early in the morning, and as we were driving west on Melrose Avenue, about a mile or so from the famed studio gate, Steve pulled out a small bottle of vodka from his jacket and took a couple of swigs. Steve had been telling me about some of the drinking binges that he and Patrick had been on in San Francisco. It shouldn't have surprised me, but I was shocked to learn that his drinking now started an hour or so after breakfast.

Once we arrived at the studio, we drove around in my truck for a little sightseeing. Steve was taking shots from his bottle in between me pointing out various places of interest and movie landmarks. When we arrived at the operations office, I told Steve to wait for me in the truck. He was slurring his speech and I didn't want anyone I worked with to see him in this shape. On our way back to my apartment Steve talked more about various drinking binges he'd been on recently. I wondered if he had remembered that we had just left Paramount Studios; he never mentioned it. He left for San Francisco a day or so later. On our way to LAX Steve said he enjoyed his stay and would return again soon. Driving back to my apartment I started thinking, *Do I really want him to return?*

MEAN STREETS

Throughout the '70s and into the early '80s, downtown Oakland was home to scores of old movie palaces, most of them leftover from the pre-World War II era, the glory days of movie-going. In those days, people dressed up for a night at the picture show; going to the movies was an event. Now, these once proud-palaces featured triple bills of mostly exploitation fare and porno. The Lux, The Broadway, Fox Oakland, Roxie; all of them were still wonderful theaters for film buffs. Those who had little concern for their safety could catch films that wouldn't dare play the cinemas in the suburbs. The Lux was a particular favorite of ours. The theater's snack bar had a window that opened to the sidewalk, so if you wanted a bag of popcorn or a slice of pizza, you didn't have to enter the lobby. Steve and I had frequented these theaters often, starting way back when we were in our early teens when we would scour the newspaper theater listings in hopes of finding some off-the-wall obscure film that piqued our interest.

We did take precautions, mind you. For starters, we knew better than to rest our heads on the theater seats for fear of lice, bed bugs or worse, but various vermin or human stench would never stop us from attending the movies. It was the Broadway Theater in downtown Oakland that screened *Valley of Gwangi*, one of the last Ray Harryhausen films. We also caught *Scars of Dracula*, one of the later Hammer films, in the same place. It happened to be one of the only theaters in the Bay Area to show these films. We had been reading about them in monster-movie magazines for months and were dying to see them. Since he lived in Oakland, Steve patronized these fading theaters often, at least when he wasn't at a bar. Sadly, due to the recent advent of cable TV and VHS tapes, these once-grand movie palaces would mostly be shuttered in the next few years. By this time in the late '70s, when Steve did attend a showing he would always have a couple of drinks first, then slip a bottle of vodka into his leather "heat" jacket, as he liked to call it, so that he could keep drinking during the movie. In downtown Oakland, he was not alone in doing this. These theaters were full of patrons drinking "bag juice" while watching the films.

When he wasn't drinking or going to the movies, Steve was running around looking for work as an extra. He lucked into his next role and he didn't have to travel very far to do it. In late 1979, famed director Richard Donner (best known for directing the *Lethal Weapon* series) brought his production of *Inside Moves* to the Coliseum. The entire film had been shooting in Oakland, a rarity since most Bay Area film shoots happened across the bay in San Francisco. One of the film's characters is a disabled basketball player hoping to make it into the professional ranks. The basketball scenes were shot at the Coliseum and called for footage of the actual Golden State Warriors playing a game, along with additional shots of the crowd and vendors. Steve stayed as close to the camera as possible and is seen in one scene briefly walking up the stairs selling beer.

Glimpsed onscreen longer was our good buddy and fellow vendor Abe Souza. Abe was something of a legend in the Bay Area vending business. He had been around for years and would continue to work well past retirement age. When it became difficult for him to walk, management bought him a motorized wheelchair so he could continue to sell peanuts, until he died in his late eighties. Abe had vended at the Beatles concert at Candlestick Park years earlier and loved to tell us, "They had them (The Beatles) in a cage! The fans were so loud you couldn't hear them, but I made a pile of money anyway."

Steve had wanted to buy Abe a hooker for his birthday one year but Abe told him bluntly, "It doesn't work anymore! It's like this (holding up his hand with a limp forefinger)! Don't bother." Abe joined us many times after the game for food and drinks. He liked to hang around us, even though we were all at least 50 years younger. Steve and the other vendors were elated that Abe was immortalized on film.

Inside Moves quickly left the theaters upon its release. The era of big-budget blockbusters had arrived with *Jaws* and *Star Wars*. Small-budget, interpersonal films would soon be a thing of the past. The film did give Steve one more thing to be proud of: he had appeared in a movie that had a score by John Barry.

Late one afternoon, not long after shooting wrapped on *Inside Moves*, Steve was barhopping by himself on Broadway in downtown Oakland. At this point in his life, Steve was fond of saying, "You drink just to get drunk, plain and simple." This day he had achieved his goal unusually early. Exiting one bar and bound for another, he left the sidewalk between a couple of parked vehicles and, without much of a glance for oncoming traffic, into the street. Then...*WHACK!* A fast-moving car hit him, sending him flying into the air and back down to the asphalt. The car sped off as Steve lay in the street, bloody and unconscious. As luck would have it, a cop witnessed the incident and immediately pulled over the offending driver a few blocks away. Steve would learn later that when the cop questioned the driver about not stopping, the driver responded with, "He was jaywalking." The cop countered with, "You still have to stop!"

The paramedics took Steve to a county hospital. With no health insurance and no money, it was his only option. Steve's right leg was badly torn up. It was broken in two spots and the skin had been scraped off around the kneecap. The doctor had to put a full leg cast on him and he was moved out of the emergency room to another room to recuperate. Later that evening, Steve was startled awake by a couple of guys rummaging through his belongings in the nightstand. In his groggy state, he started to protest, so the thieves took off and left the room, but not before stealing his pants. Fortunately for Steve, he had the foresight to keep his wallet under his pillow. It was bad enough that the hospital was filthy and smelled; now he had to contend with night raiders. At first he thought the thieves were employees, but later he figured out they were local street people who wandered in after-hours to loot the patients' rooms. Apparently, this happened on a regular basis.

After three days in the county hospital, Steve was ready to leave, but the doctors were not ready to let him go. After complaining to anyone who would listen, he convinced the staff to let him sign a release, promising to stay off his leg for a month. Steve called Patrick from his hospital bed and said, "You have to come and pick me up from this hellhole. And bring your truck."

Patrick was bewildered. "Why the truck?"

Steve answered, "You'll understand when you get here. Just come and get me. I'll be out in front."

Patrick did as requested. He spotted Steve, still wearing a hospital gown, sitting out in front of the medical center with a huge cast on his leg. "I can't bend my leg," Steve told his friend. "I don't think I can ride up front." Patrick tried to get him in the front seat anyway but to no avail, so he had Steve lie flat on an old blanket in the bed of the truck. The whole scene reminded Steve of the Laurel and Hardy short *County Hospital*. Patrick opened up the back window so they could at least converse. Steve barked out directions to his apartment as Patrick drove away from the hospital. "Pull over at the bus stop," Steve yelled out just a few blocks away. As Patrick did, he wasn't surprised to look and see they were directly in front of a liquor store. Steve yelled out again, "I'll have to owe you the money, I'm broke. But can you go in and buy me a bottle of Stoli?" He thought for a second, then amended, "Ah hell, make it Smirnoff." Patrick did as asked, surprised that Steve had now moved on to cheaper vodka.

Back inside Steve's apartment with the help of Patrick, Steve moaned on and on about his cast. It went from his upper thigh down to his foot, and at the knee, there was a removable cap. The doctor had instructed him to unscrew the cap and regularly pour some type of liquid on his knee, then screw the cap back on. Patrick almost passed out at the sight of Steve's raw, wounded knee, which had almost zero skin as he'd left the rest on the pavement outside the bar. It looked like something out of a horror movie. Steve requested a steak knife from the kitchen. To make the cast more manageable, he whittled away at the top part of the cast. He was unable to trim much with the small knife, but he was finally able to cut a substantial part of the top off with a handsaw Patrick borrowed from a neighbor. At least now he could move around a little easier.

A few days later, he complained to Patrick, "I'll never get laid with this on." The very thought of not having sex spurred Steve into creative action. He came up with a plan. He had Patrick's wife cut open one leg of his corduroy pants, then sew a wide piece of elastic into the opening. This enabled Steve to get his cast into the leg of his pants without the cast showing. I don't know if he got laid with it on, but he most likely did. He did go back to work eventually, only now with an obvious limp. It impacted his beer sales because he wasn't able to get around the ballpark as quickly; and since all the vending work was on commission, he saw his pay drop substantially.

A month or two after the accident, Steve's brother Charlie made a rare visit. Charlie was living in Florida at the time and had not seen his brother in a few years. Steve was delighted that Charlie came all that way to see him. The first night Charlie was in town they were out drinking at a bar in San Francisco when Steve exclaimed, "I want to get my little brother laid!" Charlie ignored the outburst, but the more Steve drank, the more he became focused on the mission. He finally talked Charlie into driving him in his rental car to an area of San Francisco where they could at least see the girls for hire. "I know a couple you'd really like," Steve told his brother. Upon their arrival, Steve spotted one girl he knew, so he had Charlie pull over so they could converse. Steve tried negotiating a two-for-one deal, but the woman was an old pro and firm on her price. In the end, Charlie didn't want anything to do with the hooker, so Steve convinced his brother to wait in a diner across the street while she serviced him in the car. To make matters worse, Steve had to borrow the money from his brother to pay the prostitute. And the diner he was waiting in was full of transvestite hookers, eyeing Charlie like a piece of meat. Charlie sipped on coffee until Steve could finish receiving his blowjob. It would be a long time before Charlie would visit his brother in California again.

After the accident, I told Steve I'd drive up to the Bay Area for a visit so we could catch up. I hadn't seen him in some time, although the phone calls kept me posted on what was happening with him and our mutual friends. The cast had just been removed, so I wasn't surprised when I knocked on his apartment door and he wasn't home. As always, Steve was easy to find. I knew the bars where he hung out. If he had money, he would be in San Francisco. But if dollars were scarce, I knew I could find him in Oakland or Berkeley. I found him in Bertolli's, an Italian restaurant/bar on the Oakland/Berkeley border. We had been going there for years. The food was good, but, more importantly, the drinks were cheap. You could get a triple shot of Stoli for $1.50, which even in those days was a real bargain. It was the place to go to get a heat on before you moved to the nicer places that had better-looking women. Steve was sitting alone at the bar, downing triple shots of Stoli. We said our hellos, and I took a taste of his drink and gagged, "How can you drink this?" It tasted like rubbing alcohol. He laughed. He was thinner than the last time we'd seen each other and his face was noticeably scarred from the accident. His dark complexion helped hide the scarring a bit, but it was still visible.

Since I had the car and a few bucks in my pocket, he wanted me to drive him to San Francisco. I agreed, provided we stop at Jaxx, a steakhouse in Union Square, for something to eat before we started to drink. "I don't eat food much anymore," Steve told me. "I get all my nutrients from vodka. It's made from potatoes and really contains all the vitamins and minerals I need." The statement was getting old and tired at this point. It had to be the first time in history that someone argued for vodka being a health drink. I explained to him that I hadn't eaten since I left Los Angeles about seven hours earlier and really needed a bite. "I realize that I'm a drunk," he blathered on, "but that's what I want to be at this point in my life." When I tried to tell him that he was drinking himself into an early grave, he responded by saying, "I only drink the best vodka. People die from drinking cheap booze. No one ever dies from drinking the good stuff." I'd also heard that refrain before, of course, but now it was beginning to sound pitiful, not playful. That ended my argument, but Steve relented and agreed to stop at Jaxx so I could have one of their wonderful steak sandwiches. We had been there many times before over the years. Steve also knew they had a well-stocked bar.

In 20 minutes or so we were in the heart of San Francisco's Union Square. We waited for my lunch to be served while Steve sipped on his beer, leaving the vodka behind for the time being. He told me that besides the residual problems brought on by the hit-and-run accident, he also had a few other health problems. During his last few trips to Lake Tahoe, he told me, he had noticed he had developed a bad cough that would last throughout his stay. The cough would result in shortness of breath that made it difficult for him to get air. A doctor explained that he had developed some sort of chronic breathing problem, bronchitis most likely, and suggested he should stay away from high altitudes. I also suggested that maybe he should stop smoking so much marijuana, but of course, he wouldn't consider that. "It's the only way I can sleep," he would tell me. He had also picked up various STDs from prostitutes, but those were on their way to being cured due to the help of a doctor at a local free clinic, he told me. He had also developed a severe case of hemorrhoids, which he blamed on the cold cement floor at the Coliseum. The vendors would sit on the floors, sometimes for an hour or so, playing liar's poker, talking, and waiting to be picked for work. The hemorrhoids became so painful that, a little while later during our walk back to the car, Steve froze in pain for a few seconds before he could continue.

The following day we were walking around Oakland's Lake Merritt Park, not far from his apartment. I was taking photos and talking to Steve before my long drive back home. I asked Steve to pose for a picture. While I lined up to take the photo, he stopped, smiled with that Monzelli grin, then unzipped his pants and whipped out his penis and said, "Get a photo of my dick! It should be immortalized." I did and he quickly zipped up his pants.

A few months later, Steve was back in the hospital. He had been dating a girl named Priscilla, a cute, tall blonde that I had met on a previous trip north. I figured that this relationship just might have a chance of lasting. After all, she was a bartender in one of Steve's favorite bars in San Francisco, and she seemed to really care about him. Of course, as much as she loved him, she just couldn't stand his constant drinking. When she'd finally had enough of his drunken antics, she called him up and broke off the relationship. Steve was crushed. It all came to a head one night a few days later, in the bar where she worked. Steve entered the bar, "drunk off my ass" he would later tell me. It was his intention to plead with her to call off the breakup. It might have worked if he had been sober and promised her that he would give up the booze and pot, but that wasn't going to happen. The discussion with Priscilla turned quickly into a shouting match, which ended when the bouncers literally tossed him out the door into the rainy night where he landed on his ass on the sidewalk. He was now still drunk but really pissed and wet, and he felt the sharp pain of his injured leg growing in intensity. He slowly made it back to where his car was parked, climbed behind the wheel, and drove off in a burst of speed that Steve McQueen would have been proud of. However, he didn't get very far. In an instant, he had lost control of the car and began to sideswipe numerous other cars that were parked along the street. His car finally stopped when he crashed head-on into a streetlight. The vehicle was a crumpled, smoldering mess. Steve was out cold, with blood flowing from an open wound on the side of his head and face.

The next morning he was awoken in the hospital by a police officer who wanted to ask him a few questions about the crash (turns out the streetlight he'd hit was directly in front of a police station). Steve told the lawman that a cat had run in front of his car and that he had swerved to avoid killing the animal; and being a rain-slicked street, he'd lost control, then sideswiped a few cars before smashing into the lamp post. Somehow, some way, the cop bought the flimsy explanation.

As bad as the accident was, Steve's good luck was still holding firm. Although they had checked his blood type for the required transfusion, no one in the hospital had bothered to check his blood alcohol content. But the accident left him with severe permanent scars on the side of his face and forehead; and for someone who could never pass a mirror without looking at himself, this hurt. Unlike the scars he received during the prior accident, which were minimal to his face, these were extremely noticeable, forcing him to give up some of his vanity.

One good thing did come out of the accident—he gave up driving. "I don't want to hurt anyone," he told me on the phone. "I'll keep drinking, but no more driving." Hell, he didn't need a car anyway. He could always talk someone into taking him somewhere, even a stranger. If it was a woman, he could usually talk her into driving to her house for a roll in the hay. Not long after this latest accident, Steve was riding on a bus one evening, trying to get home after a night of drinking. He was conversing with a female passenger who was kind enough to listen to his drunken ramblings. The talk went on and on about nothing in particular. Steve really wanted to get laid so he asked, "So do you want to go to your house and fuck?" She quickly found another seat on the bus. He learned from that incident to never actually ask to get laid. He was also becoming less discerning in his selection process. At closing one night while barhopping in San Francisco, he picked up a woman from some dive along Market Street. They went back to her house and fucked the night away. When he awoke the next morning he was shocked. "She was a beast!" he told me later. He was so ashamed he had sex with her that he quietly grabbed his clothes and shoes, got dressed, left the house without waking her, and ran as quickly as his injured and alcohol-wracked body could run, then found a bus to take him back downtown.

When he couldn't find a willing woman in a bar, there were always hookers. It became easier for Steve to pay for it rather than to use his old and played-out pickup lines. With his finances severely depleted, he would seek out the cheapest hookers he could find. He knew some working girls in the very rough areas of Oakland who would charge only $20 for a blowjob. Sometimes, if he negotiated enough and it was late in the night or early morning, they would accept less. At this point in his life, the idea of a relationship seemed out of the question. Steve was smart enough to realize that he was an alcoholic, a broke drunk with only a part-time job. He was also quickly approaching his 30th birthday. Now, with his scarred-up face, no car, and no hope or desire of getting a better job, he also realized that not many women would be attracted to him any longer, no matter what lie he was willing to tell them or what clever movie quote he could try and impress them with. Something had to give.

TWO FOR THE ROAD

By the time the mid-'80s rolled around, booze and marijuana were quickly becoming passé. They were the last generation's tools for catching a buzz. A new crop of drug users had what they considered a vastly superior way to get high: cocaine. Coke had taken off like no drug before, quickly becoming the substance of choice in the Bay Area party scene. It was everywhere. Gold spoons worn on necklaces had become a fashion statement for both men and women. Stickers extolling the virtues of the white powder dotted the bumpers of cars throughout the city. Cocaine was far too expensive for Steve to purchase on a regular basis, so the only time he'd get it was when he could score a small amount from one of the vendors at the Coliseum. He also had plenty of friends, and friends loved to share their cocaine with him. Unfortunately, the drug had a bad effect on Steve, causing him to become angry and combative. Alcohol and marijuana made him jovial—cocaine could make him lethal. Fortunately for those around him, Steve quickly realized what was happening and stopped. When he was on the powder, he would pick a fight with anyone he could get his hands on, like some kind of possessed demon. But after one too many cocaine-fueled fights, Steve decided he'd had enough. He simply stopped using without a second thought. Fellow workers at the Coliseum continued to offer him the stuff, but he refused. Alcohol and marijuana were more humane, Steve decided. Those drugs didn't change him into a wild beast.

Late one night I received a most unusual call from Steve. "John, I'm fucking a grandmother, can you believe it?" he said. I responded with mock incredulity and then waited for the full story. It turned out Steve had met yet another woman in yet another bar in San Francisco, but this woman was considerably different from all the others. Brenda was older than Steve by about ten years and she had a good, steady profession; she was a registered nurse, and was in fact a grandmother, albeit a young one, not the grey-haired granny-type of my first impression. During my next visit to the Bay Area, I was amazed to see Steve sporting a new look. Gone were the old leather "heat" jacket, blue jeans, and Hawaiian shirt. He was now wearing slacks, a dress shirt, and a sport coat. *Brenda must really have her hooks in him*, I thought to myself. We met her downtown at the medical office where she worked. Her shift had ended and we all went out to dinner. I was encouraged to see that Steve was at least eating on a regular basis again (he appeared to have gained some weight since the last time I'd seen him, a good thing).

It didn't take long to see that Brenda was a most unique woman. Her most striking aspect was that she was almost as big as Steve. She was built like a bull, and with her short, cropped hair she looked like an ex-Marine drill instructor. During the meal, I noticed she was the take-charge type and liked to argue with Steve anytime she disagreed with him. With her predilection for conflict, I thought that if they ever got into a fistfight, she would probably kick Steve's ass and remain smiling throughout. She delighted in telling me how they had met. She had walked in the door of one of Steve's favorite bar hangouts. After making small talk, she'd asked what he did for a living, and he told her he was a movie producer. She immediately countered with, "No you're not! You don't have any of this!" She rubbed her thumb and forefinger together to show she was talking about money. "Producers must have a lot of this." She did it again. "What do you *really* do?" Steve confessed and told her the truth about his job at the ballparks and his work as an extra. Brenda smiled and said, "Now we can talk. Sit down." She was on to him immediately. She might have been drawn in by his charm, but she saw something else.

The relationship turned serious quickly. Brenda, to Steve's delight, could match him drink for drink in the various bars they frequented in San Francisco. Her only complaint about barhopping with Steve was walking into a place and figuring out Steve had fucked just about every woman in there. There was another benefit to Steve for dating Brenda. Since she was a registered nurse, she was a walking vending machine for prescription drugs. She had been a user herself for years, and now she was able to keep Steve supplied as well. Vodka and marijuana were still his drugs of choice, but depending on what Brenda brought home after her shift, Steve would down the pills and chase them with Stoli.

Brenda had a horrendous temper. She made fighting an art form. Something as simple as asking her if she wanted to get a bite to eat could set off an argument. She could and would start a shouting match with almost anyone, over just about anything, didn't matter the place or time. One of the people she fought with most was Patrick. She didn't like Steve and Patrick hanging out in bars without her. She thought Patrick was a bad influence who encouraged Steve to drink to excess; Patrick thought she was evil. Ultimately Steve saw less and less of Patrick. They would talk occasionally on the phone but over time even the calls became less frequent. He had no desire to hang with the two of them, and Steve quickly became inseparable from Brenda.

Brenda could match Steve shot for shot at the bar. She could drink all night and wake up bright-eyed in the morning with help from numerous cups of Steve's extremely strong coffee (courtesy of his Italian Moka coffee maker) and still hold down her job as a nurse. This impressed Steve and made Brenda an attractive mate. The fact that she made a good living was a bonus. She also became a buffer between Steve and his father. The Old Man was not accustomed to strong-willed women taking him on. Their arguments were loud and frequent and often ended with Brenda shouting The Old Man down. The Old Man, ornery as he was, was no match for Brenda. The Old Man was slowly losing his control over his son and he didn't like it, and he didn't like Brenda either.

Brenda had been living in San Francisco for a couple of years before she met Steve, but she was originally from San Diego. She had family down there, including a husband she was long separated from. Since becoming a grandmother, she had longed to be back in southern California to be with her daughter and grandson. After almost a year of dating she gave Steve an ultimatum: move with her down to San Diego or split up. Brenda did what I thought was impossible; the ultimatum worked and Steve agreed to leave the Bay Area and move with her to Carlsbad, a 30-mile drive north from San Diego. Brenda's daughter Patty and her son Justin (Brenda's grandson) lived in Oceanside, a couple of miles north of Carlsbad. Steve was excited when he called me with news of the move. "John, Carlsbad is great. The town looks just like the one they used in *Invasion of the Body Snatchers*." And indeed, he was correct, it certainly did. The switch from the cold and windy fog-bound streets of San Francisco to the sunny warm beaches of Carlsbad was a surprisingly easy transition for Steve.

Brenda found them a modern two-bedroom apartment within walking distance of the beach. Steve quickly acclimated to the Southern California beach lifestyle. During the day Steve would lay out on a towel and work on his tan, and in the evening tell Brenda that he had been out looking for work. Brenda finally caught on one day when she was strolling along the beach with a friend during a lunch break from work. They stopped to take in the ocean view when Brenda pointed out to her friend what she thought were two good-looking black guys. As they walked closer to get a better look, Brenda realized that one of the guys was actually Steve. His daily trips to the beach had made his dark Italian complexion darker than ever. Brenda kept her temper in check as they continued their walk. There would be plenty of time that evening after a hard long day at work to discuss this matter yet again with Steve. Yet another screaming fight ensued that night, with Steve promising to actually start looking for employment the following day.

With Steve only two hours away from my home in Los Angeles, we were able to see each other frequently again. With the recent advent of home video, I would bring along VHS tapes to his place and we would sit around and watch movies and drink beer until late in the night. By this time, Steve had sold off his comic book collection and a big chunk of his movie poster collection to Patrick. He still had a few greats left (*Casablanca*, *The Big Sleep* and *To Have and Have Not*) that adorned the walls of their apartment, along with numerous photos Brenda had taken. Brenda's hobby was photography. She was quite good and loved to show off her work. One of her pet projects was to take pictures of Steve's penis from every conceivable angle. She printed out the photos on contact sheets but fortunately, these photos were not on general display. Steve was uncomfortable, understandably, when she would show off the pictures, especially to her female coworkers from the hospital, but she was proud of them and took her hobby very seriously. Over time I got used to Brenda's frequent tirades, which for some reason were rarely directed toward me. I don't know why this was so, but actually, she seemed to like me. I couldn't return the feeling but I was always pleasant toward her. Over time I had developed a system whereby the two of us could converse without it leading to an argument. The two of them began hosting frequent barbecues, where Steve delighted in making the largest hamburgers known to mankind.

The food would precede a showing of some obscure movie Steve had just purchased, along with an ample supply of beer.

Even as he approached his late thirties, Steve was still always up for an adventure. Carlsbad was only an hour and a half from the Mexican border and Steve had been there many times over the years, as he loved it for the cheap booze and cheaper hookers, and because it was a favorite hangout of director Sam Peckinpah, our old "friend." Some of the whorehouses were too sleazy even for Steve. Once in Tijuana, he met a hooker in a bar and made a deal with her for a blowjob. She then took him to the backroom for service. In the dimly lit space, there was a long bench full of other guys, sitting with their pants around their ankles, getting blown by other hookers. A flimsy cardboard partition separated Steve from the other customers. Steve, drunk and quiet, sat among the other guys as she went to work on him. The hooker complained that Steve was taking too long. When he did finally shoot his load, she tossed him a wad of toilet paper for him to clean up with and she quickly darted back to the bar looking for yet another customer. Steve vowed never to go back to that particular bar.

About a half-hour south of Tijuana lies the beach town of Puerto Nuevo. Dubbed "Lobster Village," it was basically a dirt cul-de-sac that ended at the Pacific Ocean. The dusty road was lined with restaurants overlooking the ocean that specialized in lobsters and margaritas. They were very tasty lobsters, and they came with warm handmade tortillas to wrap around the meat. We would drive there often and fill up on the tasty crustaceans and tequila. During one particular trip, Steve drank so much that Brenda had forbidden him to drive. The car was stuffed full because Brenda had brought along two friends from work, as well as her estranged husband and her five-year-old grandson, Justin. Steve squeezed into the back seat and quickly passed out, while

Brenda drove the group back on the dark winding road to the Tijuana border crossing.

The border was always a difficult drive. Cars backed up for miles as border agents decided which vehicles to stop and search before being allowed back into the United States. A two-hour wait was the norm even in the middle of the night. The waiting would be consistently interrupted by people knocking on the car windows, trying to sell you everything from piñatas to piggy banks shaped like Elvis or Batman. One fellow selling two-foot-long crucifixes banged on the car particularly hard and woke Steve from his alcohol-induced slumber. Steve stared at him, rolled down the window, and asked for a closer look at the crucifixes. The vendor thought he had a sure sale when Steve asked in all seriousness, "How much for the Jesus on a stick?" Brenda screamed at Steve as I apologized to the vendor and then tried to explain to Steve what a gross insult he had made to the fellow, if not the entire country, which was about 90% Catholic at that time. Steve smiled and replied, "I've got to take a leak." Traffic wasn't moving an inch, so Steve bolted out of the car into the mass of vehicles and vendors. After a few minutes, he returned, having relieved himself somewhere, and promptly passed out again. Brenda inched the car forward when suddenly we heard *wham wham wham*, which we quickly realized was coming from the fist of a Mexican police officer pounding against the car window. I promptly rolled down the window and Steve woke up again just in time for the officer to point a finger at him and yell, "You! I saw what you did! Come with me, you're going to jail." Until that moment I had never seen the look of fright on Steve's face.

Brenda took control of the situation immediately and shouted back to the officer, "Good, take his ass to jail, it's where he belongs."

The officer agreed and yelled back, "Get out of the car now, I take you to jail!"

After Brenda yelled at Steve to get the fuck out because they wanted to get home, Steve exited the vehicle and the officer put him in handcuffs. Steve pleaded with Brenda, knowing full-well what a jail in Tijuana would be like. "I don't want to go to jail, please help me," he said.

Brenda would have none of it and snapped back with, "That's where you belong."

Having heard the stories about the Mexican justice system, I asked the cop, "Do you have to take him to jail? Can we just pay you the fine?"

The officer calmed down and came back with, "I don't know how much the fine is, maybe $150 or $200, and I don't have a receipt."

Brenda yelled again even louder, "I'm not paying any fucking fine!"

"We don't need any receipt," I told the officer. I asked around and no one in the car had any money except for Brenda's husband, who found $20 in his pocket. I made up the difference and handed the cop $200, which he quickly stuffed into his pants. He told Steve never to pee in the street again. Steve promised he wouldn't. The officer took off the handcuffs and Steve got back in the car and promptly passed out yet again.

Steve's inability to get a job would be the source of endless arguments. Brenda made a good living and had a strong work ethic, but she wanted Steve to pitch in too. According to Brenda, he would stay up to all hours watching videos (purchased with money she earned) and then sleep most of the morning, then it was off to the beach for a suntan. She worked double shifts so his laziness really pissed her off. One Saturday afternoon it all came to a head. She let Steve have it with an assault of verbal threats. She insisted that he get a job immediately, and to drive the point home she picked up his VHS Collector's Edition copy of *Dr. Zhivago* and threw it on the kitchen floor, jumping up and down on it and crushing it into bits and pieces. She had given the two-tape set to Steve as a gift some months before. *Dr. Zhivago* was one of Steve's favorite films, and now it was a crushed mess on the kitchen floor.

Steve, who had spent the morning and afternoon drinking and smoking dope, flipped out into a state of rage, screaming and threatening Brenda with physical harm. Fearing for her safety, Brenda ran into the bedroom and locked the door. Steve pounded on the door and when she yelled for him to stop, he began breaking the door down with his feet and fists. She grabbed the nearby phone and called the police. By the time the cops arrived, Steve was completely berserk. He answered their knock at the front door but when he saw the cop, instead of calming down he leaped at the officer, grabbed him around his head, and wrestled him into a headlock as they both fell to the ground. Steve was on top of the poor guy, in total control, but within a few seconds, he snapped back to his senses and realized it was not a good position to be in. He let go of his grip on the cop, which was a very good move since the backup officer had just arrived, and he had a police dog with him that he was just about to release on Steve.

Steve surrendered peacefully after that. They cuffed him and tossed him in the back of a police cruiser. Brenda ran outside during the commotion and yelled out a chant of, "Take him to jail! Take him to jail!" What a scene. A female backup officer had also arrived. She opened the rear door of the patrol car to take a quick look at Steve and saw him sitting inside with his hands handcuffed behind him and his body secured by a seat belt. "So you're the guy who likes to beat up cops? We don't like that around here," she said. She pulled out her baton and slammed the end into Steve's stomach. Steve wouldn't give her the satisfaction of screaming out in pain; he held it in and sat quietly even though the pain was intense. He knew good and well that he was fucked.

In North County San Diego they had a way of dealing with people who beat up cops. They tossed Steve in the section of the jail reserved for black inmates. The cops hoped they would "take care" of Steve and beat him to a pulp. It was not to be. It turned out that some of the inmates just happened to be from Oakland, and after plenty of conversation, they discovered that Steve and a couple of the other guys inside had mutual friends. "We're going to let you have a bed," one inmate told him. "We never let white people have beds, but you're okay. However, if a brother needs a bed, you'll have to give it up." As far as Steve was concerned, this arrangement worked out perfectly. Nevertheless, Brenda went ahead and pressed charges for assault. Since Steve couldn't make bail, he sat in jail; days became weeks. He spent Thanksgiving behind bars. He would explain later, "It really wasn't too bad. They had a turkey and everything."

A month passed and Brenda still refused to put up the bail money. I didn't have the amount he needed, nor did any of his other friends he called in the Bay Area. The Old Man was always the last resort for a pinch, but this time even he had had enough of Steve's erratic behavior. Steve stayed the duration. When he finally was sentenced, he got time served along with a year's worth of weekly Alcoholic Anonymous meetings, weekly anger management meetings, and three years of probation. Brenda refused to let him back in the house. With no place to go and so far from San Francisco, he moved in with me. I was renting a small house in the San Fernando Valley. Steve talked about giving up drinking and becoming either a stuntman or a pool man, but professions require work and planning. It was easier for him to watch laser discs from my collection and smoke dope and drink vodka all night long than to plan a money-making future.

After having him as a roommate for a month or so, he announced he was moving back with Brenda. It wasn't a surprise. Their nightly phone conversations became longer and longer, with less and less yelling as the days went by, and a lot more crying, at least on Steve's part. Steve desperately needed to be with Brenda. The relationship was much more complex than I had initially realized. It was not just boyfriend and girlfriend; she was a mother figure and even a father figure as well.

Once back in Carlsbad with Brenda, Steve found a job. He became a waiter at a popular beachfront Mexican restaurant. He called me with the good news but was perplexed that so many employees were named Jesus, as in Jesus Christ. He had seen their names on their time cards. I had to explain to him the proper Spanish pronunciation of the name, then it all made sense to him. With the extra money he made at the restaurant, one would think he would begin to contribute to the bills around the house. But not Steve. Now he could afford a higher class of hookers. Steve was now very happy to be back with Brenda. He deeply loved her, and she gave him stability he had never had in his life. However, having sex with the same woman every night was just not appealing to him; he needed a choice of women, and hookers offered the best and easiest option when it came to variety. Steve was impressed with the quality of the hookers so close to his apartment. I explained to him that since he was so close to the Marine base at Camp Pendleton, it actually made a lot of sense. A light went off in his head and he agreed. He was also enthusiastic that so many tourist women visited the restaurant where he worked. He was getting laid so frequently that it was almost like being back at Palo's Place.

In the end, the stint in jail didn't seem to faze him much, but he would have to follow the dictates of the court. It was a routine he wasn't used to, but he would have to follow them if he didn't want to go back to jail. As mentioned previously, one of the conditions was to attend weekly AA meetings. The idea originally seemed like a colossal waste of time to Steve, but he did as he was ordered. At one of the early meetings, he met a fellow named Tom who was also a film buff and a lifelong alcoholic. Tom had been sober for a couple of years and gave the credit to AA. They hit it off immediately and Tom eventually became Steve's "sponsor." A sponsor is your helper—he's been there, heard it all, and tries to guide you along the path of sobriety. After long talks with Tom, serious introspection and many meetings, Steve finally agreed to give up drinking. Or I should say he was at least willing to give it "one day at a time."

HEARTBEAT

I couldn't keep my thoughts to myself any longer; I had to speak my mind. "Steve, this is very weird," I began. "Here it is, a warm summer Saturday night, and we're walking past beautiful women, streets lined with bars and nightclubs. But instead of stopping in and having a couple of drinks, listening to music, and talking to the ladies, we're going to Alcoholics Anonymous. We should be on Union Street, looking for bars and nightclubs filled with beautiful women, and getting a heat on."

Steve realized I was fucking with him. He just smiled, then repeated his oft-used phrase: "Times are changing," a nod to Sam Peckinpah's 1969 film *The Wild Bunch*. We were now inside an old church in Carlsbad, the location of the first of many AA meetings I would attend with Steve. As he was a so-called "newcomer" then, it was Steve's job to arrive early and make the coffee. He took the appointed position with the utmost seriousness. «They like their coffee strong, and that's the way I make it," he boasted as he heaped loads upon loads of ground coffee into a giant stainless steel coffee maker. The meetings gave him a sense of community outside of a bar; and perhaps more than that, a sense of purpose. The people at the AA meetings depended on Steve to have their coffee ready before every meeting. He didn't want to disappoint them (and no one wants to deny a roomful of recovering alcoholics their coffee). At that point, he had given up drinking for a couple of weeks. Brenda demanded it as one of her stipulations for getting back together and letting Steve move back in. Smoking weed was still okay with her, as she did it herself, but he was to have no more booze, not a drop.

At the meeting, I met Tom, Steve's sponsor. Like so many in AA, Tom had been through the wringer, once living on the street and begging for spare change to spend on liquor. Now through the help of the program, he had been able to stay sober and turn his life around. Tom took it upon himself to try to keep Steve off booze. Amazingly, it seemed to work. Tom's street smarts and wisdom cut through any bullshit or flimsy excuses for drinking that Steve might come up with. Plus, Tom was also somewhat of a film buff, which helped them bond. Steve had finally come to realize just how much damage liquor had done to him over the years, and now he was strongly determined to stay off the stuff. As he had been drinking for so long, and drinking was such a big part of his life, I couldn't imagine a completely sober Steve. It seemed impossible to me, and I waited for what I assumed would be the inevitable leap off the wagon.

As strange as it sounds, a sober Steve was just as much fun as a drunk Steve, maybe even more so. Someone once referred to Steve as a man-child—we even used it as his nickname for a while—but once he got off the sauce, Steve developed a rather different, more mature personality. But he was no less fun and/or funny to be around. After a while, AA became very important to him. He attended meetings nightly at the beginning, making certain never to miss a day. Instead of collecting videotapes, he now collected the chips they give out for staying sober: 24 hours, 30 days, 60 days, 90 days, etc. He loved showing off his growing collection of chips almost as much as he loved showing off his collection of movies.

Brenda enjoyed the sober Steve too, and they seemed to be enjoying a sort of domestic tranquility. She could still be set off into a rage on a moment's notice, but not as often as in Steve's drinking days. Brenda continued with her photography. She set up a darkroom in the spare bedroom of their apartment. She loaded the room with the latest equipment. Her cameras were all top of the line in these pre-digital days, and she would shoot photos incessantly. She continued to photograph Steve's penis at every opportunity. I never understood why his dick fascinated her to this extreme, but it did. Since Steve used his dick so often and with so many different women, maybe it should be immortalized in photo after photo. During most visits, she'd delight in telling me how many times that preceding week Steve had asked for a "sympathy fuck." According to Brenda, Steve was far ahead in that category.

Sobriety certainly seemed to agree with Steve, and his life became almost idyllic. Between June and August, I would drive down on Saturdays, and we would spend most of the day at the beach. By late summer the ocean was so warm that we would waste away hours in the water, swimming and talking film, or countless other topics. Steve had lost none of his excellent swimming ability. He would take off and go beyond my line of sight, then swim back, laughing about how far he'd been out to sea. One of the reasons he loved the beach at Carlsbad so much was that the local power plant was within sight. It reminded him of the hideout used by Dr. No in the first James Bond film of the same name. He delighted in telling anyone he was with, or met at the beach for that matter, that Dr. No's hideout was just a few miles away. The barbecues continued, too, albeit with some changes. "The hamburgers are normal size now," he'd say. "Since my sobriety, I don't grill the giant burgers any longer." That was fine by me. I could never finish one of his behemoth burgers anyway. Of course, there were still the occasional outbursts from Brenda, but even she was beginning to calm down, to take stock of her life, and realize she had a lot to be happy for.

Steve was in as stable a situation as he'd ever experienced before in his life. He would spend his free time recording movies off cable, building his collection of VHS tapes. Like many film buffs, he'd stopped seeing many newly released films, instead escaping to the older films readily available on any channel. Hollywood's Silver Age had come to an end with the dawn of the 1980s. It was becoming harder to love cinema with what was currently coming out of Hollywood at the time. It was easier for me to track down the harder-to-find movies to rent in Los Angeles, and then bring them down during my visits. Hollywood was now the mecca for video rental stores. When Steve would come up, we would spend hours at various video stores, renting films to later duplicate at home. It was a dream come true for film buffs. Who would have guessed you could own so many films at such a cheap price? We had purchased many films on 16mm, 8mm, and even a few on 35mm throughout the years, but film was extremely pricey to purchase and cumbersome to view. Home video was a film buff's dream come true.

Steve was pulling in more money at his restaurant job. Management liked his sense of humor, and he was a good worker. They increased his hours and gave him better shifts. He enjoyed the banter with the customers, especially the women. He enjoyed it even more after making a deal with the bartender. Steve would put in his drink orders and the bartender would not ring them up. The customers would tip Steve extra for the free drinks, and he would split the profits with the bartender. The duo started to make some good cash with Steve's idea; that is, until the manager found out about the scheme and promptly fired them both. Steve didn't take the firing too seriously, but Brenda threw a fit. "Get a fucking job" was her frequent refrain, always stated in a loud shrill voice that she could do to perfection. Steve would occasionally go out and look for employment, but only half-heartedly. He would rather be at the beach or an AA meeting.

One thing Steve did take very seriously was his love for Justin, Brenda's grandson. I found this surprising since Steve had no previous experience with small children. Justin was six years old when Steve and Brenda made the move to Carlsbad. Steve loved playing with Justin, and it was evident that Justin loved Steve. Steve shared his love for movies with the young boy; and although he was perhaps too young to enjoy most of them, it didn't stop Steve from trying to give him an education in classic cinema. Problems would arise from time to time with some of Steve's choices in films. He loved to show Justin the classic Universal horror movies, the ones that Steve had grown up with like *Dracula, Frankenstein, The Wolfman,* and their various sequels. Eventually, Justin came to believe that the Wolfman himself lived just outside the parking lot at Steve and Brenda's apartment building, in some bushes near the walkway. He would scream and cry when it came time for him to walk on the path to get in the car. There was also the issue at preschool—Justin started biting the little girls in class on their necks, just like Dracula did. The school suggested Steve stop showing the kid vampire movies, but Steve refused. He reasoned that these films had no effect on him as a young boy and he couldn't understand the staff's concern. He did sit Justin down and explain to the young child that the monsters in the films weren't real and couldn't hurt him. It seemed to work, and fortunately, the kid stopped sinking his teeth into classmates.

Sharing his love for cinema was one thing, but now Steve wanted to share another one of his passions with Justin: driving. As someone whose glove compartment was often stuffed full with overdue traffic tickets, Steve was the last person who should have been teaching anyone the rules of the road, especially if the person hadn't reached the age of seven yet. Case in point: Steve and I picked up Justin from his mother's house one morning. She lived about a half-hour north.

The plan for the day was to deliver Justin back to Steve and Brenda's apartment and then, once Brenda's shift was over, head south to the San Diego Zoo for a day of fun. Simple enough. Once we were inside the car with Justin, Steve announced proudly, "I've taught Justin how to drive, he's really good." Personally, I didn't want to experience just how good a driver the seven-year-old was, but I was outvoted. As soon as we were out of sight of his mother's house, little Justin scooted over onto Steve's lap and grabbed ahold of the steering wheel.

"Lift the turn signal," Steve commanded. Quick as a flash young Justin would signal for a turn. Then Steve would tell him, "Right turn now," and Justin would crank the wheel with all his strength (if this older model car had power steering, it certainly wasn't very effective), and with a little help from Steve, he would complete the turn. I had to admit that even though he could barely see over the dashboard, he did a fine job under Steve's watch. The little boy certainly had a lot of enthusiasm, and you could see the love he had for Steve. He would listen intently to every instruction Steve gave him. Within a few blocks of Steve's apartment, Justin jumped out of Steve's lap and Steve told him with all sincerity, "Don't tell your grandmother that you've been driving. She wouldn't understand." Justin agreed.

When Brenda arrived home, we all headed out to the parking lot and she insisted on driving. The zoo was about an hour away. While zipping down Highway 5, Justin, who was unbuckled sitting between Brenda and Steve, suddenly dove for the steering wheel and clutched it with all the force he could muster while screaming, "Me drive! I wanna drive!" Brenda tore the child from the wheel and screamed at Steve, "He's been driving again! I told you not to let him drive!" Steve tried to explain that Justin was a very good driver, but the incident put her in a foul mood for hours. The trip to the zoo was ruined before we even arrived. Brenda spent the shortened time we did have there either yelling at Steve or not talking to him at all.

Steve was not into metaphysics, not in the least, but he became convinced that Justin was the reincarnation of Steve McQueen. He would stop in mid-sentence and tell me that Justin had just given him a "McQueen look." I frankly didn't see it, but Steve was certain of it. He became totally obsessed by this when he found out that Justin was born on November 8, 1980, the day after McQueen had died. Justin's father was out of the picture for the most part. The father lived by himself, not far from Justin's mother, but he didn't seem to want much to do with his son. On those rare occasions when he did show up, he would bring gifts of toy guns, sometimes half a dozen or more. This pissed off Brenda and Steve to no end. Both of them refused to let Justin bring any of these toy guns into the apartment, but at his mother's place, they were everywhere. Steve increasingly became a surrogate father to Justin, which delighted both Justin and Steve. It became obvious that Steve had become the kind of father that Justin should have had in the first place.

"How do you like this shirt?" Steve said one day as he greeted me at his apartment. "Brenda bought it for me."

"Looks great," I responded. (It's difficult for me to get excited over a shirt, especially when it's worn by a guy, but I digress). I was thinking that perhaps dressing well goes hand-in-hand with sobriety. Even around the apartment, Steve had stopped wearing blue jeans and T-shirts and now looked the part of a successful yuppie—except he still didn't have a full-time job. I came to realize that along with the sobriety, my friend had matured. He still had his overriding love of films, but now there was no need to imitate the on-screen antics that he watched, only view them, discuss them, and share them with friends. His videotape collection continued to grow and grow. His taste in film was always eclectic and would run the whole spectrum of cinema. Once at a Suncoast Video store, he grabbed a tape from the rack and yelled over to me for all to hear, "John! Have you seen *Bloodsucking Freaks*?" I answered in the negative. A few minutes later he yelled out again, asking if I'd seen *Going Places*, a French film that he considered among his all-time favorites; I hadn't seen that film either. He seemed to gravitate toward films about antisocial behavior. Back in the days when we hung out at Cinema Treasures in San Francisco, Patrick would enjoy conversing about "films featuring cruds." Patrick and Steve shared an affinity for these movies. Steve introduced me to films I had never heard of, films that only the most ardent film buffs had seen. He could talk in-depth about the German Dr. Mabuse films or Japanese noir movies. I always wondered how he found out about those titles—mostly from Patrick, I assumed—but however it was, I was always grateful that he shared his knowledge.

Rummaging through video stores had become a favorite pastime of ours. By the mid to late 1980s, films on VHS tape flooded the marketplace, causing prices to drop. Back when they first debuted, a feature film on videotape ran $100 and sometimes more. We were amazed at the number of films that would line the shelves of various video stores that you could rent for a few bucks. Going to video stores in the local malls served another purpose as well—we could check out the women in the mall. This worked especially well in the winter when the beaches of Carlsbad would be mostly vacant. Steve had slowed down his sexual urges since his sobriety. He told me one day of his past: "I was a human penis in those days, that's all I was." A good line, I thought, and not from any movie that I was aware of. He still loved to look at women, and would occasionally find a hooker, but for the most part did not stray from Brenda. He certainly never considered leaving her for another woman, even though some of his friends wished he would have.

One day, Steve had somehow learned that Desi Arnaz (from *I Love Lucy* fame) lived just a few miles away, and acquired the actor's home address. Steve thought we should go by and pay him a visit, just like the old days when we would knock on the doors of various celebrities. It sounded like a good idea at the time, so we got into his car and made the drive to Del Mar. We drove up to the driveway to Mr. Arnaz's home and then sat for a while in Steve's car. Actor Rebecca Schaeffer had been murdered by a stalker some months previously. Celebrity stalking had been in the news a lot lately and the longer we sat in the car, the more we rethought our plan. I had met Mr. Arnaz at a book signing in San Francisco about ten years earlier, so I had my autograph. Instead of knocking on his door, I took a couple of photos of his beautiful home, and then we decided to move along. Times had indeed changed.

For the first time in Steve's life, a relative calm had set in. Carlsbad is a place where people go to retire, or at the very least vacation, laying on the sandy beach and soaking up the warm sun. The lifestyle was as far away removed from his life in the Bay Area as one could possibly get, and to my amazement Steve loved it. His friends at AA became his social network. Brenda's brash personality kept most of his old friends from visiting. Patrick called on occasion, but visiting was out of the question. Brenda still worked double shifts at the hospital, so Steve could have peace and quiet for long stretches of time. Tom, his AA sponsor, became his close friend and primary source of guidance, the older brother and father figure he had never really had. Steve had always looked at movies for guidance.

Because of Tom's advice, and because it is one of the tenets of AA, Steve began contacting people he had wronged over the years and apologizing for his past behavior. The calls were mostly to scorned women. To the ones he was able to contact, he apologized for any hurt he had caused and told them that now that he was sober he was a changed man. Most accepted his *mea culpa* and the calls were a catharsis for Steve, as they did much to relieve the guilt he'd carried around since the '70s. In addition to the women, he also informed me that he wanted to contact National Screen Service to apologize for stealing their garbage so often those many years earlier, but I talked him out of that. That was going too far; it *was* just garbage, after all, and who did we hurt? He also had an intriguing idea. He wanted to make a movie in the style of *Citizen Kane,* in which his previous girlfriends would face the camera and tell their stories about having known Steve. He wanted them to be brutally honest about their relationships. Unfortunately, this never went beyond the talking stage. That was too bad, because I thought it would make a very interesting movie, and an easy one to shoot now that videotape was cheap and readily available.

Tom had been worried about Steve's health ever since they had met. He had noticed Steve's deep cough and the fact that he had been losing weight rapidly. Steve had abused his body for years and had rarely visited a doctor. Steve had a laundry list of ailments, some active and some in the past, from various sexually transmitted diseases to the chronic deep cough that worsened when he went to high altitudes. The cough was so severe that he couldn't sleep during his later excursions to Lake Tahoe; he would spend the night in bed hacking away and gasping for air. He also still had that horrendous case of hemorrhoids, and I'm certain his liver had taken a severe beating. Steve must have felt something was amiss too because he listened to Tom and scheduled an appointment for a complete physical. He left his apartment extra early the morning of the exam because he wanted one last trick with a hooker he liked who worked at a nearby motel. He figured he owed himself one last fuck before he straightened out completely.

Steve called me late in the evening a few days later. He had just received the results of the physical and he was fighting back tears. "John, I have AIDS," he told me. I was in disbelief. Stunned, my own tears began to flow. It was impossible. *Not Steve,* I thought. Not much was known about AIDS in 1989 other than that many people were dying from it, mostly gay men. It was considered a death sentence during these early years. "Don't tell anyone," he asked. I told him I would not. "Brenda's having a test tomorrow, just to make sure she's okay." My only response to this terrible news was to tell him to "go back to drinking, just stay drunk." How else could someone face this? He quickly responded, "You don't understand. I drank because I was afraid. I'm not afraid anymore. I want to face this head-on and sober." *Afraid?* I thought. Had I missed something all these years? Afraid was the last thing Steve had been. Hell, his adventurous spirit and no-holds-barred way of living were inspirations for how I lived my own life. He had taught me the importance of living life to its fullest and not being scared of the consequences. His confession about being afraid rang loud in my ears. What could I do for my friend? As Steve fought back tears, he confessed that he felt so bad for the hooker that he had fucked on the way to the doctor's office. "I hope she's okay," he cried. "I hope so too" was all I could manage to say. After we said our goodbyes, I called a friend and told him what Steve had said to me. I couldn't hold his secret in; it was just too much horrible news for me to contain. I had to talk to someone about it. I knew my friend could keep the secret.

I drove down to Carlsbad the following weekend to spend the day with Steve. I hadn't seen him for a few weeks, but he looked the same, except for a rash on his face. We took a drive to the nearby mall, the same mall where he would walk around endlessly anytime

Brenda demanded that he go look for a job. He never did ask anyone for work, but he could convince himself that he was looking. While on the freeway headed to the mall, he pointed out the motel where he had met up with the prostitute on the day of his physical, then he confessed: "Brenda has AIDS too." I was stunned but not surprised. "She doesn't have it as bad as I do. It's not as advanced," he explained. Steve again asked that I not tell anyone. AIDS was considered a disease akin to leprosy at the time; you became a social outcast. He was adamant about keeping both their diagnoses a secret. At the mall we made our way to Suncoast Video, checking out the women as we walked. I pointed out a couple of cuties for Steve and asked him, "How would you like to have them?" He answered with, "I can't anymore, that's all in the past. And you know what? I really don't miss it."

I tried to visit Steve almost every weekend. It was only an hour or so south from L.A. in good traffic. The visits became predictable: the mall in inclement weather and a stroll on the beach when things were better. As the weeks progressed, I could see the toll the illness was taking on my friend. Steve began to lose more weight, the color of his skin darkened to a charcoal color, and his energy level lessened. Brenda mentioned that when he had a bad week, he would always seem to rally for my visits. On occasion, I would bring along my video camera and tell him I had a role in one of my movies for him. He still loved being in front of the camera. Back when we were teenagers we had shot an 8mm sound home movie entitled *An Afternoon With Steve and John*. Now some twenty years later we shot a sequel. I cut both films together, and a few weeks later, Steve, Brenda, and myself watched the finished product. It was a delight to sit around and watch us as young guys in the Bay Area and then see us so many years later in Carlsbad.

In the early years of the AIDS epidemic, adequate medications were simply not available. Newspapers were filled with front-page news of statistics of deaths and the amount of people becoming infected with this horrible disease. Talk radio was filled with scare stories regarding this rapidly spreading disease. Some people thought you could catch AIDS by just being around those affected. Others talked about the possibility of quarantining people with the disease. Steve's health was on a fairly steady and rapid decline. The doctors had him on loads of experimental medications but to no avail. As per our usual routine, one Saturday morning I drove him out to the mall again. This time it was a struggle for Steve to get out of my car. He apologized for having to use a cane to walk. I told him there was no need to apologize, but that he should get a wolf-head cane like the one Lon Chaney, Jr. had in *The Wolfman*. The walk to the entrance was slow and difficult for him. When we finally made it, Steve turned to me and in a weak apologetic voice said, "I can't make it, I'm sorry, take me back home." Back inside the car, he apologized again. I told him not to bother; we could go back to his apartment and spend the rest of the day watching movies. He agreed to that and then asked for a favor. "Could you buy me a shake from In-N-Out Burger? I'm broke, and it would make me feel better." So I did.

Back at his place, watching a film he remarked, "It's sometimes hard for me to see the TV." He had started wearing glasses sometime earlier, but he said they didn't seem to be working any longer. I turned off the TV so that we could talk, but after a few minutes, he fell asleep on the couch. While he napped Brenda brewed some coffee for us. She told me that Steve had been napping a lot, but that the naps only last about 10 or 15 minutes and that I should hang around. We were finishing our coffee when Steve awoke. Steve loved listening to talk radio; he would listen late into the night, gathering all sorts of information. Steve had heard on one of the shows that soon there will be large-screen televisions, flat ones that you could hang on walls.

I had heard nothing about this, but he swore that they would soon be available. Convinced that this would be the solution to his failing eyesight, he made Brenda promise that she would buy him one once they were on the market. But later when we were alone, she told me that they were both broke, and that Steve didn't have much time left.

I thought this was a particularly cruel end for my buddy Steve, the ultimate film buff, now dying a slow death. Soon he would be unable to do anything else besides lay on the couch, blind, unable to watch the movies he so loved.

Amazingly, Steve would not complain about the situation. He remained hopeful that there would be a future for him.

NEAR DARK

Steve knew his days were numbered. He just hoped those days numbered in months and not weeks. Still, he mustered enough energy to throw one final bash. He called me with the news: "John, I'm having a Super Bowl party. Brenda will cook some food and I'll have some friends from AA here. I want you to come."

Wow, I thought—a dilemma. "Steve, I've never been to a Super Bowl party in my life," I told him. "In fact, I kinda pride myself on being one of the few Americans who has never even seen a Super Bowl. I can't break my streak now."

He responded bemusedly but weakly with, "Don't be an idiot, come to the party." I agreed, provided I could leave before the end of the game, so that I could at least say I'd never watched an entire Super Bowl. That was fine with him.

The day of the big game arrived and Brenda was on her best behavior. She had all the requisite Super Bowl delicacies: chips, fried chicken, cookies, etc. Tom and four or five other AA members were there too. No alcohol was being served, of course, but Steve did say I could bring some beer for myself. I told him I could do without a beer; and besides, how many dry Super Bowl parties are there in southern California? I figured we could relish the fact that we were the only one. While we were watching the game, Steve told me he didn't attend as many 12-step meetings as he used to. He was still strictly adhering to the tenets of AA, but it was becoming too difficult for him to get out of the house. It was very nice of his AA buddies to show up for the party, I thought. The talk was, for the most part, on the game itself, all aspects of the game. These people really knew their football. They were talking way over my head. The only thing I knew of football was from the three seasons I worked at the Coliseum watching the Oakland Raiders. For one afternoon Steve had a respite from his disease. There was no talk of doctor appointments, blood tests, or new experimental medications that were on the horizon; no talk of AIDS at all. It was just a bunch of guys yelling instructions through a television set and telling each other about all the mistakes the players and the referees were making on the field. It was almost like the old days when he would get together with friends in the Bay Area and watch sports, only this time there was no gambling or boozing. Steve didn't seem to mind when I excused myself and left for home during halftime. I don't think his AA friends understood why I would be leaving in the middle of the game, but I saw no reason to try and explain. Back home I couldn't explain it to myself.

Shortly after Steve's admission that he had contracted AIDS, it was announced in the press that Los Angeles Lakers star Earvin "Magic" Johnson had also acquired the dreaded disease. The country was in shock; the disease seemed omnipresent. If the invincible Magic could get it, then anyone could. AIDS was constant front-page news. Rallies and marches in support of a cure were held in most major cities. This was of little help to Steve. Most anyone living with the disease was treated as a pariah. The public's cry for action did keep AIDS awareness front and center, at least during these early years of the outbreak. For all her faults, Brenda made certain Steve received the best medical care possible. She shuttled him back and forth from physician to physician, clinic to clinic, using her contacts in the healthcare field to find him the best doctors and treatments. No one could have done a better job caring for Steve than Brenda. Unfortunately, there was little the medical community could do for him. Physicians were only beginning to understand how to treat AIDS and Steve had an advanced case, having contracted the virus long before testing positive. He was prescribed various medications, but they seemed to have little or no effect. In the early years of the epidemic, AIDS was considered a quick death sentence. Fortunately for Brenda, she showed no outward symptoms of the disease, at least in the beginning.

Before long, Steve began to feel like a pariah. Despite his best efforts to keep his affliction a secret, word of his condition spread. Most of the friends he had made around Carlsbad, with the exception of his friends at AA, stopped calling. No one wanted to be around someone with AIDS. Aware that Steve would eventually require in-home care, Brenda decided to find a larger place for the two of them to live. Despite Brenda working double shifts at a local hospital, mounting medical bills meant money was in extremely short supply. She realized Steve would never be able to work again. Shortly after his diagnosis, Steve had been working part-time as a waiter at a posh local resort. We took a drive through the grounds one day; it was a large, beautiful place. He told me how nice the staff was to him and how much he enjoyed working there. One night while assigned to a banquet, he spilled an entire pitcher of icy water into a woman's lap. She became irate, yelling at him and calling him an idiot. The pitcher had been too heavy for him to hold. He realized at that moment that he didn't have the strength to continue working. He quit before he could be fired.

Brenda started an intense search for a new home. She knew exactly what she wanted, and visited places endlessly during her off-hours. After a couple of weeks, Brenda found the perfect home. It was a small, older residence situated on a bluff overlooking both Carlsbad and Oceanside, with the Pacific Ocean in the distance. The living room was large enough to accommodate a hospital bed, which Brenda knew would soon be needed. During my first visit, I told Brenda that it was one of the most peaceful homes I'd ever been in. She decorated it beautifully, and of course, there were movie posters on the wall. This was quite an upgrade from the apartment they had lived in before. Brenda was doing a wonderful job caring for Steve.

However, out of the blue, there were two more people who suddenly wanted to help, at least in their own twisted ways. After living almost his entire life in Oakland, Steve's father, The Old Man, decided to take his wife and move the almost 500 miles south to Carlsbad. They said they wanted to contribute to the care of their disease-stricken son. Brenda, being a registered nurse, had been doing a fine job, and I didn't see that she needed the help. I had my problems with Brenda's personality, as almost everyone did; but since the onset of Steve's illness she had really come through, and I admired her for her willingness to fight for him. With her explosive temper, I had expected her to put a bullet in Steve as soon as she learned he'd given her AIDS. She did not; instead, she quietly accepted her fate. Though she was not nearly as ill as Steve, her medical background meant she knew all too well what was in store for them both.

When The Old Man arrived, it was just like old times. Brenda and Steve's father had fought constantly when they lived in the Bay Area, separated by the Bay Bridge; now they were separated by a mere ten-minute drive. The Old Man and his wife had rented a condo in Carlsbad, then he quickly made the appropriate drug connections before starting to weasel his way back into what was left of his oldest son's life. The battles between Brenda and The Old Man resumed immediately. He was convinced that Brenda was the cause of all Steve's problems, medical and otherwise. He couldn't or wouldn't face the fact that his son had contracted AIDS most likely via his sexual escapades, or perhaps the blood transfusion following his car accident. He accused Brenda of not only causing his illness but also of not knowing how to properly care for him. It became so intense that she barred him from their house at one point, but later rescinded the ban after she had some time to cool off. Steve's mother, still the quiet one in the family, remained in the background, smiling but rarely talking, except to agree with whatever The Old Man was yelling about. It was The Old Man who Brenda always had to fight with. He treated Steve's illness as if he had some type of severe cold, one that could be cured with a visit to a proper doctor and, oh yes, with Brenda moving away for good.

The Old Man openly blamed Brenda for all of Steve's problems. He was convinced that she was responsible for infecting Steve—not the other way around—and he wasn't the only one. Some of Steve's friends in the Bay Area thought the same thing. Since she was working in the medical field, they figured she had most likely been infected with AIDS on the job. Due to her hot-headed temperament, she was an easy target for blame. The Old Man had always been incensed that Steve had fallen in love with such a strong-willed woman; he preferred the silent and complacent type. During one relatively calm period, when everyone held their tempers at bay, Steve's father held a backyard barbecue, complete with plenty of liquor and dope. The Old Man was the only one using or drinking at this point (Brenda was also clean), but that didn't stop him from staying well-stocked with narcotics. Steve, who was becoming frailer every time I saw him, was having trouble walking and was now using a different cane (alas, still without a wolf-head handle) to slowly move around. The Old Man was tolerable at dinner, still loud and obnoxious but bearable. I never understood why he had to shout every time he talked. Maybe I should have asked him.

After the barbecue, Steve, Brenda, and I walked to our cars. Steve had given up driving and was slowly making his way to the passenger side when he stopped suddenly and turned to me. "John, can I give you a hug?" he asked.

"Of course," I replied. Strange, I thought, but this was the first time I had hugged my friend of so many years. During the embrace, I noticed his weight loss was much worse than I had previously realized. He was all skin and bones, frail and cold.

The following weekend I sat and talked with Brenda while Steve slept. He slept a lot in those days, no longer just quick cat naps. After an hour of conversation, we finally got around to The Old Man. "Did you notice his living room last week?" she asked. I didn't know what she was getting at. "There was only one photo of Steve in the whole place, and the photo they did have was of Steve on a pony when he was seven!" There were at least twenty pictures of his brother Charlie, she said, like a fucking museum of Charlie memorabilia. There was even a large oil painting of Charlie hanging on the wall as you entered the condo, done by one of Charlie's girlfriends. She was correct, spot-on correct. I hadn't even noticed. "That's why Steve has acted out so much through the years. He wanted the attention and he never received it from his parents, the people who matter most to a young child," she told me. "They worshiped Charlie and ignored Steve." This obvious truth, one I was completely ignorant of, poured over me like ice water, opening up all my senses. I felt like crying for Steve. I could feel the pain my friend must have felt. The more I thought of what she said, the more it made perfect sense. This talk, and others to be held in the coming weeks, brought Brenda and me closer than we had ever been. Her insight was keener than mine. I felt ashamed for having bad-mouthed her to Steve's friends on more than just a few occasions.

The Old Man was convinced Steve had a treasure trove of film memorabilia worth a fortune. He may have at one point, but that had been years ago. The Old Man was oblivious to the fact that Steve had been selling off his memorabilia for years. How else could he have afforded those endless nights of partying with hookers, bar tabs, and restaurant bills? But now he was broke and most of his collection was a distant memory. To make sure he would wind up with what he thought was a memorabilia gold mine, The Old Man went to a lawyer to try to get conservatorship over Steve's affairs, since Steve and Brenda had never been married. It had nothing to do with any concern for his son's health or well-being; he just wanted to be sure that Brenda didn't get anything that belonged to Steve when he died. Steve was too frail to deal with this, but he did know what his father was trying to do. Brenda went to see a lawyer as well. She had a good case, but she was near-broke and couldn't afford to pay the attorney.

One day while visiting Steve he asked me what I would like from what was left of his collection. I pondered the question, then quickly picked out a one-sheet poster to *Hell's Kitchen*, a 1939 Warner Bros. film starring the Dead End Kids and Ronald Reagan. I'd owned the poster at one point in my life, but sold it when I had needed some quick cash years earlier, and had regretted the decision ever since. I was overjoyed to have it back in my possession. I would not part with it again. I also took a box of 16mm Laurel and Hardy films that Steve had owned since we were in high school. Just after graduating, Steve would rent out the films and his projector to local pizzerias—along with himself as projectionist. He didn't make a lot of money, but the audiences enjoyed the films while eating their pizzas. I donated all the films to The Sons of the Desert, the Laurel and Hardy fan club that I had been a member of for years. Steve had joined me at some of the club meetings in Los Angeles. He enjoyed going but always had to get a buzz on first—vodka and Laurel and Hardy, go figure.

While we talked about splitting up the rest of his collection, Steve managed to say in a very soft voice, "Do you want anything else?"

I thought for a second and said, "Could I also have one of your shirts?"

He smiled. "I'll tell you what. I'll give you a shirt, along with my heat jacket. I call it my heat jacket because I always had a heat on when I wore it. You might as well have it. I won't be doing any more drinking." I put the Hawaiian shirt along with the heat jacket on a hanger. When I arrived home, I hung them in my closet. Steve had talked about spreading out what was left of his collection on the floor and letting his friends pick out what they wanted, but as his time grew to a close this never happened. He did have one very collectible item left, his one-sheet poster for *Casablanca*. He knew it was worth at least a couple thousand dollars, but he had treasured the poster for years and refused to part with it. He had bought it while in high school for five bucks. He wanted his brother to have it, and I thought that would be the perfect person to own this one treasure that was left in his collection. I knew The Old Man would sell it as quickly as possible if he ever got his hands on it.

Due to Steve's rapidly deteriorating condition, Brenda made a difficult decision. She told her daughter that Justin should not be around Steve any longer. At this time there were wild tales of how easy the AIDS virus could spread. She didn't want to jeopardize Justin's health or have him frightened by Steve's frail appearance. His mother made up an excuse as to why Justin couldn't visit his favorite "uncle" anymore. Brenda would continue to visit Justin alone at her daughter's apartment. Steve understood and accepted the policy, but it must have been especially painful for him. He loved that little boy and talked about him often. Steve didn't mention the pain it caused him, but during my next visit I found him lying on his bed digging through boxes of photos that Brenda had taken through the years; he was looking for a photo of himself and Justin. Steve found a particularly poignant one of him sleeping soundly in bed with Justin sitting next to him staring at his face. Steve put the photo on his nightstand next to his bed as a remembrance of a much happier time.

Sadly, the fight over Steve's possessions dragged on. The Old Man's lawyer sent Brenda letter after letter, demanding that she turn over various items. I found the whole fight to be like some kind of surreal circus, with the ringmaster being played by The Old Man. Steve had bounced a $300 check on me only a few months before he became seriously ill. I knew he had no money, and very little in the way of possessions. The Old Man thought otherwise. His hatred of Brenda was intense and bordered on psychotic. He wanted to cause her harm any way he could find. Brenda had given up taking her own required medications as the side effects were just too much to bear. She wanted a clear head to deal with Steve and with the ongoing battle with The Old Man. She had cut back her hours at work, partly due to Steve, but also as a result of her own failing health, although she wouldn't admit it. She laughed off her rapid weight loss to friends, attributing it to a new diet.

Eventually, her months-long fight with The Old Man over Steve's belongings came to an end—she lost. A judge granted Steve's parents conservatorship over all his possessions and medical decisions. The possessions were all he wanted, not the responsibilities. He left the care of his son in Brenda's capable hands. In the end, Brenda had neither the funds nor the willpower to sustain a protracted legal battle. She reluctantly relinquished the rights to all of Steve's meager collection of memorabilia to The Old Man. The Old Man was now confronted with the knowledge that once Steve died, he would own what little was left of his collectibles. Not long after the court ruling, The Old Man and his wife showed up at Steve and Brenda's to collect what was theirs. Brenda barely said a word; she was more concerned about Steve's failing health. The items, which at one time meant the world to Steve, were meaningless to her at this point. Steve was aware of what was going on, but he just didn't have the energy left in him to fight what would be the last fight with his father. By this time, Steve was largely bedridden. He slept most of the day and night, with occasional trips to the couch where he would nod off and sleep some more. He had shrunken down to less than 100 pounds from his peak of 180 in his prime. His skin had darkened considerably, and he was covered with sores of all types. Brenda continued to care for Steve. She was careful to always change his bandages herself; she didn't want me or anyone else to come in contact with any of his bodily fluids. Her training as a nurse was invaluable. Brenda moved Steve into the spare bedroom, where it began to resemble a high-tech hospital room, except for the few movie posters on the wall that The Old Man had left hanging.

Even in this weakened state, Steve had a final plan to screw The Old Man. He would marry Brenda. Brenda wanted this too, but since she was still legally married, she would have to get divorced first. She knew her husband would sign the papers, but Brenda didn't think Steve had much time left. Still, it did seem the best solution to cut off The Old Man for good. Steve was closing in on his 40th birthday, and Brenda said if he made it to that milestone, she would have a very quiet get-together for just a few of his close friends to mark what would surely be his last birthday on Earth. Steve wanted to hang on but I secretly wished he wouldn't. It was all so painful to see. No one should suffer like this, I thought. Brenda discussed the matter of divorce with her husband, and he readily agreed to sign all the papers required to start the proceedings. Unfortunately, in California there is a six-month waiting period before a divorce is officially granted. Brenda knew that Steve wouldn't live another six months. After considering the long waiting period, she informed her husband that she would not file the papers after all.

Not knowing how much longer Steve had to live, I wanted to talk to him about something that had been on my mind for some time. I was not much of a believer in the afterlife at the time, and even less of a believer in ghosts and spirits and such. However, if one person would try and come back from the dead and create some mischief for me, I knew it would be Steve, so I asked him bluntly one day, "Steve, if you can come back after you die, would you just leave me alone? Go ahead and bother anyone else that you want, but not me. I don't want you fucking with me."

He laid his head back on his pillow, smiled, and then said, "Yes, I won't bother you, don't worry." I felt better. He had created enough mischief alive; I didn't even want to consider what he could do in the afterlife.

With Steve fading rapidly, I would drive down every weekend to see him, if only for an hour or so. Seeing the deterioration of my close friend was almost unbearable, but I came up with a plan to ease my struggle just a bit. On my way south I would exit Beach Boulevard in Huntington Beach and stop by Ken Crane's. In those days they were one of the largest retailers of laser discs in the world. I would buy one disc before every visit. They were expensive, but it made me feel a little better driving to his house. It gave me something fun to look forward to. Steve had a laser disc player of his own, but he was beyond his movie-watching days at this point. I had to wait until I returned home to watch the movie. I sat by his bedside one afternoon with a laser disc I had just purchased. It was a *Way Out West* starring Laurel and Hardy from 1937. "Steve, they just released a new Laurel and Hardy film," I told him.

Steve didn't open his eyes very wide, but he did grin and said softly, "You can't fool me. Laurel and Hardy aren't making new films."

I smiled and told him, "Okay, you've got me there. It's an old film new to laser disc!" He grinned some more. He still had his sense of humor.

During Steve's final weeks, he would lay in the hospital bed that Brenda had set up in the living room. With the curtains open you could see the beautiful rolling hills of Oceanside and Carlsbad, along with the Pacific. Steve had completely lost his vision, but he had seen the view many times before. Brenda and I made calls to his many friends, telling them that they should come by and say their final goodbyes. Only a very few of his old friends from the Bay Area made the trek south to visit him. Eddie stopped by one weekend while I was there. I hadn't seen him since the Coliseum days. I talked to Eddie about the old days in Oakland, when his side business was renting out his vast 16mm porno film collection for parties. It was a lucrative business; he had made some good money at the time, much more than Steve had renting out his Laurel and Hardy films at pizza restaurants. Eddie was paid in cash; no one would dare write him a check. He was now a police officer in the Bay Area and very happy in his new profession.

Eddie was in shock over Steve's condition. The last time they had seen each other was in an Oakland dive bar shortly before Steve had moved south. They had spent the evening tossing back shots, celebrating Steve's impending move. Eddie spent the afternoon at his friend's bedside, wiping away tears while trying to converse with Steve, who was mostly unresponsive. He left shortly afterward to visit The Old Man, and then to head back to the Bay Area.

On one of his last nights alive, Steve struggled to whisper something to me. I leaned in close. His voice was dry and weak. "Dean is coming tomorrow, he has a cure," he said softly. Dean was a friend from high school who, like Brenda, had become a nurse. Also like Brenda, he had a serious pharmaceutical drug habit; but unlike

Brenda, his habit required a needle. He would always have plenty of prescription drugs with him, and he brought a generous amount when he arrived the next day, but no cure. Dean was so whacked out on drugs that he was barely able to get a complete sentence out. He sat at Steve's bedside, talking as well as he could to his old buddy. Steve drifted in and out of consciousness. A few hours later Dean stumbled back to his car and drove north.

Patrick would still call occasionally from San Francisco. Steve loved the calls and wanted Patrick to visit, but Patrick's hatred for Brenda was such that he would never consider it. There were other Bay Area friends who I thought should at least call and offer support; but due to the reputation of AIDS during that time, it frightened many, so most just stayed away. Fortunately, Steve's sponsor Tom and other friends from AA never stopped visiting.

One morning after arriving from Los Angeles, I sat next to Steve's bed. His eyes were closed but I could tell he wasn't sleeping. The radio on his nightstand blared a talk radio program. He gave me a weak "hello" when he realized I was present. I responded with, "I'm going to leave if you don't turn off Rush Limbaugh."

Steve grinned, showing off his yellowed teeth and parched dry lips and mouth, and responded with a quiet, "He makes me laugh."

I smiled and told him, "Okay, I'll stay a while longer, but just because we're friends."

Listening to both Limbaugh on the radio and *Pee Wee Herman's Playhouse* on television brought him some enjoyment. They were his constant companions during this dark time.

THE LAST DETAIL

Charlie, Steve's younger brother, came to see him in Carlsbad not long after his diagnosis. The two rarely saw one another in person but had kept in regular contact via phone and mail. Charlie, who I assumed had his own issues with The Old Man, moved to the East Coast after high school and never looked back. The few times we had talked over the years, I can remember him referencing his father's strange behavior and leaving it at that. It was their father, after all, not mine, so I decided it was not my place to question his antics or ask for explanations about his bizarre behavior. At the time of his visit, Charlie was working in New York as a regional booker for a chain of movie theaters. Talk about a dream job: it was his responsibility to attend film screenings and recommend which movies should be shown in the company's theaters.

"It's a great job for someone in their early twenties," he was fond of saying. Charlie was now in his mid-thirties, so he fully understood the dilemma. He and Brenda grew closer after Steve learned he was HIV-positive. Since Steve was often too sick to take a call, it was Brenda's job to update Charlie on his brother's worsening condition. One day Charlie asked, "Should I fly out for a visit?" Brenda responded, "No, he probably won't make it much longer. You might as well wait for the funeral." Charlie agreed to stay put.

A couple of days later, on an extremely hot Thursday afternoon, Brenda called me with the news I'd been dreading to hear. She told me my best friend was at death's doorstep. Steve, only 39, so full of life since the day we'd met in elementary school, had been slipping in and out of a comatose state for over a week, and now his body was finally shutting down. There was nothing left for the doctors to do; it was only a matter of time until the end. I told her I would be driving down the following day.

I arrived early the next morning. Brenda, worn and tired, greeted me at the door with deep, dark circles under her bloodshot eyes. She was keeping the house near-silent; no TV, no movies. Steve was right where I'd seen him last, lying completely still on his hospital bed in the middle of the living room. Brenda kept every curtain open so she could see the beautiful landscape that surrounded them, the green rolling hills, the clear beautiful blue sky. Normally the television would be blaring, but not now; these were solemn times and their house reflected it. Brenda explained to me what Steve was going through, that he could die at any moment, and that we should watch over him constantly. She instructed me on how to hold up his head and let him sip from a small cup of ice water every 30 minutes or so. He was completely unresponsive, except for his parched lips that moved slightly when he would take those tiny sips of the ice water.

Brenda told me that Justin had celebrated a birthday the day before. I felt sorry for the young boy. Steve was the one adult male in his life who truly loved him, tried to give him positive guidance, and that all ended. I was grateful to Brenda for having made the difficult decision to cut off contact between the two while Steve still had the outward appearance of being healthy. The young boy should never see him like this. I hoped that Justin would remember Steve as he grew older and remember how much love Steve had for him. In these final hours, I sat down beside Steve's bed and talked to him quietly; except for a few grunts, he did not respond. Steve's skin was turning a dark grey color and he was losing more weight. Steve was in some far-off place; I hoped it was pretty there, like one of those perfect scenes from the films we loved so much as kids. He had wanted so much to make it to his 40th birthday, but that was still two weeks away and I knew he wouldn't make it.

Convinced Steve was spending his final days on Earth, Brenda made the house as peaceful as possible. She opened up all the windows, letting the warm outside breeze enter the home; she then put some of Steve's favorite movie soundtracks on the CD player. The end of his life was now being scored by some of his favorite film composers, such as John Barry, Jerry Goldsmith, Ennio Morricone, and Bernard Herrmann. She had set the volume very low, but loud enough to fill the room with this great music. Later that morning, The Old Man and his wife came by for a quick visit. All of us moved to the backyard so as to not disturb Steve with our talking. A short time later Eddie arrived for another visit. He had been driving all night from the Bay Area for one final visit with his old buddy. As The Old Man talked and we listened, I thought to myself, as I had many times before, *Why do you always have to be so damn loud?* With his constant laughing and loud, boisterous talking, he seemed oblivious to his son's situation just inside the house. He must have been in some deep denial. For The Old Man, it seemed, it was just another day.

The three of them (The Old Man, his wife, and Eddie) eventually took off to grab lunch. Brenda and I went back inside to check on Steve, and Brenda started cleaning the kitchen. It must have eased her pain as she cleaned constantly. I stood over Steve's bed watching him, lying motionless and with labored breathing. I spoke softly to him. "It's a good day to die," I told him. I had remembered that line from *Little Big Man* (1970). I also remembered that Steve never did the expected. He would only do what he wanted, on his own terms, dying included. The longer I sat at his bedside, the more I came to realize that Steve does not intend to die today. As the sun began to set, Brenda closed the living room windows and the curtains and said she needed a drink. I agreed.

Brenda had by this time been off her medications for months. She said they were screwing up her head and that she needed to be clear and alert, especially during these final months. She had been Steve's total caregiver and was doing a wonderful job of it. She wasn't a good sleeper, to begin with, and now with all the added stress she wasn't sleeping at all. She needed a break. She called The Old Man and asked for a favor and the old codger finally stepped up to the plate. He agreed that he and his wife would watch over Steve this one Friday night while we went out to dinner. There wasn't really much for them to do while we were out, except to lift his head and give him the ice water. Brenda told them she would tend to the dirty work, cleaning up his bodily fluids and such, when we returned. The Old Man and his wife arrived a while later. Brenda filled them both in on giving Steve the ice water, then she turned on the TV and we said our goodbyes. She was looking forward to one night off.

The restaurant was a loud and festive Mexican place, crowded with locals ready to party the night away. It had been weeks since Brenda had been out to eat. We both ordered margaritas, quickly finished them, and immediately ordered another round before ordering our meals. We sat quietly, staring at each other, and then we talked a little about Steve. We both prayed that the end would come quickly. The rest of the conversation was about everything except Steve and The Old Man. We were oblivious to the noise around us. As we finished our food we called for another round of drinks. The alcohol didn't seem to have the desired effect on either one of us. Strangely, it had almost no effect whatsoever. The reality of what was happening could not be masked, even with three (or was it four?) margaritas. We had been away from the house longer than we had realized. I remembered the act of eating, but couldn't remember what I ate. What did I care? A shot of tequila sounded like a good idea; maybe that would work since the margaritas had failed. I suggested the shots but Brenda said no, we should get back to the house. Maybe Steve needed us. The Old Man had my pager number, I thought; if anything had happened, he surely would have buzzed me. But Brenda was convinced that we needed to get back.

When we arrived at the house, Steve's parents were watching television in the living room. Brenda asked how much water they'd given Steve and The Old Man's wife replied, "Oh, we didn't give him any. We figured we would let you do it." Brenda was furious. The truth was that his own parents were scared to touch him. They wouldn't even lift his head and give him water. "Get out of my fucking house now!" Brenda screamed. "You don't give a fuck about your son!" I was very familiar with Brenda's boisterous tirades, but I had never seen anything like this before. She yelled at the top of her lungs but she was coherent and screamed the truth. Steve's parents didn't even care enough to give him life-giving water in his final days. They both beat a hasty retreat out the door. I don't think I'd ever seen The Old Man speechless. His wife mumbled something unintelligible, and they both were gone in a flash.

Brenda was shaking visibly. She fell silent as she wiped Steve's face with a damp cloth and gave him the ice water he sorely needed. I stood in silence watching her. I couldn't believe what I had just witnessed. How could two parents totally ignore their dying son? A short while later, Brenda calmed down enough to ask me a very serious question: she asked me what I thought about her plan to end Steve's life. At the time, the very beginning of the AIDS crisis, it was not uncommon for friends or relatives to end the suffering of their loved ones during their last days. Newspapers and talk shows were full of stories about euthanasia. Although it was still illegal, it was understandable to those of us who had witnessed such extreme suffering. "What the hell are they going to do to me if I get caught?" Brenda asked. I did not want Steve to suffer any longer, but killing him? I could not answer the question.

Brenda, after a few minutes of discussion, made up her mind to end Steve's life, to put him out of his misery. She would wait to do it until I was back in Los Angeles the next day, far from the scene of the crime so I could not be implicated. I couldn't discuss it any further for my own protection. I totally understood her decision, and I told her I would remain silent on it. But he was my friend, and I couldn't talk any longer about ending his life. It was too much to ponder. I told her to get some sleep and we could talk about it in the morning. She was beyond stressed and slightly drunk, not a good time to make such a heavyweight decision. Brenda agreed and asked me if I could watch over Steve that night. She wanted to take some heavy-duty sleep medication so she could get a good night's rest, and I agreed. I slept in Steve's old room with the door slightly ajar, only about 15 feet away from his hospital bed. I kept the light on to read for a while.

The walls of his bedroom were covered with the few movie posters still in his collection, mostly Bogart and Cagney gangster films, and a 14x36 insert poster of *The Westerner* from 1940, starring Gary Cooper and autographed by its screenwriter, Niven Bush, to Steve. Bush was the landlord of an apartment building where one of Steve's former girlfriends lived during the San Francisco days. Niven Bush loved to talk film with Steve, and Steve loved to listen to his stories about working during the golden age of Hollywood. Also hanging on the wall was his autographed photo of Steve McQueen he had obtained on the set of *The Towering Inferno*, along with a photo of Steve and Robert Mitchum taken at the San Francisco Film Festival. They both looked so young and happy. The Old Man had by then taken possession of most of Steve's other posters, including the crown jewel of Steve's collection, the *Casablanca* one-sheet. Steve, of course, had wanted his brother to have it. Lying in that dark room just steps from my dying friend, surrounded by those posters, I was overcome with emotions, but I felt at home.

At some point in the middle of the night, I began to hear a moaning sound coming from Steve. I don't know if it woke me up or if I even been sleeping at all. I'd kept the bedroom door open in case I needed to hear something, or more likely nothing at all. The moan was an eerie deep-from-the-lungs type of sound. The sound grew louder. There was no way I would be able to sleep now. I just laid there in bed, listening. It was a sound I'd never heard before, not even in the movies. Steve didn't sound like he was in pain, so I didn't want to bother Brenda. I was hoping that Brenda wouldn't be awakened by the sound; I knew she needed her sleep desperately.

Early in the morning Brenda walked into the bedroom and was at my bedside. "How long has Steve been making that noise?" she said. She sounded pissed.

"I don't know for sure. It started sometime during the night," I said.

She tried to control her anger. "It's a death rattle. You should have let me know. It's the sign that Steve's body is shutting down. I'm going to call an ambulance." She phoned the ambulance but it was two or three hours before it arrived. This upset her even more. Once paramedics did arrive, she sounded like a doctor, barking specific instructions at them. The paramedics initially wanted to resuscitate Steve but Brenda screamed "No!" enough that they finally listened to her. It was Steve's explicit instruction that he was to be kept comfortable, and under no circumstances were medical personnel to perform life-saving measures.

We both separately followed the ambulance to a hospital in San Diego. It was next to a freeway that Steve and I had driven on numerous times on our trips to Mexico and Lobster Village. When we arrived, the staff set Steve up in a room and hooked him up to some IVs to keep him pain-free and hydrated, but nothing more. Brenda and I sat next to him until the early evening. There was no way of telling how long Steve could hold on now that he was under hospital care. To my relief, Brenda's plan to end Steve's life proved unnecessary. His remaining hours were now in the hands of the hospital staff. Brenda and I sat next to Steve's bed, talking quietly. She said that the end could still be a few days away and that I should return home to L.A. and get some rest. I said my goodbye to Steve and thanked Brenda for all she did for my friend and left the hospital for the three-hour drive home.

The following day, a Sunday, Brenda called and told me that there had been no change in his status. For some reason, Steve was hanging on much longer than the doctors expected. She assured me that he was out of pain and now it was just a matter of time. Less than 24 hours later, Brenda called again. "John," she told me plainly, "Steve is dead." I was able to get something out like, "At least his suffering is over," knowing full well that Brenda's suffering would continue down the same road. Brenda made the obligatory calls to Steve's family and friends to spread the word of his passing. She then began to plan for the funeral.

It was Steve's wish that his funeral would resemble an Alcoholics Anonymous meeting. He wanted testimonials from members and friends. His sponsor, Tom, presided over the meeting/funeral, which was held in a small church in Carlsbad. The church was almost full, with the majority of the attendees being AA members. Patti, his former girlfriend from San Francisco, flew down for the service. I had not seen her in years. Also making it down, his high school buddy Dean, and Steve's brother Charlie. No other friends from the Bay Area made it to the service. Also conspicuously absent were Steve's parents. The word was they were planning their own funeral for their son, a service without any input from Brenda.

The members spoke eloquently about how Steve had brought much humor into their lives, but also about how he helped them in their efforts to quit drinking. The tributes were touching and heartfelt. Steve had touched many more lives than I could have ever imagined. One by one, people approached the microphone and spoke of their love and admiration for Steve, and the positive influence he had had in their lives. I had no idea how important he had been to the AA members that spoke. They talked about how helpful he was, how much he made them laugh, changes in their lives they'd made because of Steve's guidance and friendship. Before long it was my turn to speak. I had nothing prepared, but I had to say something about my friend. As I took my place behind the lectern and in front of the microphone, I looked down and noticed that the box of tissues was empty. "This isn't fair," I said while holding them up. "I'm going to need some of these." I told the audience of our long friendship, of the countless memories we shared together. "I have known Steve for 26 years, and during those many years there were good times, some bad times, and during the end, many sad times, but never in all those years were there any dull times," I said. The service wrapped with a singer performing the saddest rendition of *Send in the Clowns* that I have ever heard. It tore at my heart, and I'm certain it did the same for most people in attendance.

After the service, Steve's ashes were scattered off the Carlsbad coast. Brenda and I along with Charlie and a few others drove to the beach. We parked next to the restaurant where Steve had once worked and walked out onto a jetty, and there we scattered some roses in the ocean in Steve's memory. That beach was his favorite, among the many wonderful beaches of southern California. I told Charlie of the many hours Steve and I had spent in these waters during the hot summer months. I also pointed out to Charlie the nearby power station that Steve had convinced Justin was the home of Dr. No. He agreed that it actually did look like the set from the film.

The day after the funeral, The Old Man, with court order in hand, removed all of Steve's remaining belongings from Brenda's home, leaving her with nothing that had once belonged to Steve. A couple of weeks later I received a frantic call from Steve's dad. He was angry and abrupt. "John, I know you have Steve's poster collection. I want it or I'll sue you!" I couldn't believe my fucking ears. He was convinced that I was holding some treasure trove of classic movie posters that would bring the asshole untold wealth. I tried to stay calm and explain, "He had nothing. He had sold most of his collection off years ago." He would have none of it; he was yelling that I was a liar and a thief, and that he would immediately contact his attorney and then contact the police and have me arrested. I slammed down the phone and immediately picked it up again to call Brenda, but as I was dialing I could still hear The Old Man yelling at me. The line had not disconnected. I yelled at him to get off the fucking phone and slammed it down again. The second time worked. I never did hear from his attorney or the police.

A few days later Patti, Steve's old girlfriend from San Francisco, called me and I filled her in on The Old Man's threats, thanking her for coming down for the funeral. She told me of a strange thing happening at her office the previous day. She had been sitting at her desk, high up in an office building in downtown San Francisco. She had been sitting quietly working away on a project when suddenly, for no apparent reason, her bra became unfastened. It was embarrassing and she said this had never happened to her before. She said she had been sitting completely still. She had no explanation at all for this happening—until she realized it was Steve's 40th birthday. She was convinced that it was the ghost of Steve coming back for one final squeeze. I guess she'd never had the talk with Steve about not returning to haunt her after death.

Brenda's health failed dramatically in the months after Steve's passing. We would talk on the phone occasionally, but I didn't see much of her after the funeral. I guess it was just too hard since Steve had been the glue that held us together. When she became too ill to care for herself, she moved in with her sister and mother, both of whom moved to the Carlsbad area after Steve's death. They both cared for her, as she had cared for Steve. She lived for 18 months after Steve's passing. Brenda's sister had told me that there would be a memorial service for her some time in the future. If there was, I was not informed.

I had not spoken to The Old Man since the phone incident. I knew he couldn't care less about Brenda's passing, but I did want to talk to him and clear the air of the bad feelings between us. Having known both him and his wife for the majority of my life, I didn't want that phone call to be our last conversation. When I called to say hello, he snapped a cold, "What's up?" I tried to break through his icy exterior, but he would have none of it. He was still angry and didn't want to talk to me, so I simply hung up on him mid-sentence. I never spoke to him again.

I thought I had dealt with Steve's premature death fairly well. I was comforted by the knowledge he was no longer in pain, and that he had faced his fatal illness with much courage and strength, frankly much more than I could ever muster if the same had happened to me. I was also very grateful to Brenda. She had taken such good care of my friend. I still felt guilty for having bad-mouthed her over the years and wished I'd taken the opportunity to make my peace with that fact before she died. She was there when it counted; she could have spent her final months complaining about Steve, and how he was responsible for her having to face death at a young age, but she didn't complain, ever.

I would think of Steve often following his passing, always in some warm and humorous way. I remembered his wild antics and the way he turned his life around in such an honorable way. I would be comforted by all these memories. Not long after Brenda's death, the Robert Redford-directed film *A River Runs Through It* was released. I went to see it with my friend Annalisa. She had never met Steve but knew of his passing, and certainly knew of him from the many stories I had shared with her since we had met. We saw the film at the AMC Theaters in Century City. I loved going to the outdoor mall where the cinema was because it was the location used for the filming of *Conquest of the Planet of the Apes*. More often than not while walking around the mall, I would journey across the bridge used in the movie and shout out, "All right, fight like apes!", a line used at the dramatic conclusion of the film. It was something Steve would have done. Steve and I had seen the film during its first run, years earlier at the Egyptian Theater in Hollywood.

Annalisa and I lined up at the box office and I bought our tickets, then we entered the theater and sat there quietly enjoying the film, as I had done so many countless times in the past, in so many other countless cinemas. The film told the true story of Norman Maclean, a quiet, studious young man; and his hard-drinking, hard-gambling brother, who always had a smile on his face and a positive attitude no matter how grim the situation. The two dissimilar characters have one thing in common: a love of fly fishing. The sport kept them connected through good times and bad. At the end of the film, when the narrator, now an old man, speaks of the passing of his brother, his parents, and the many other important people in his life, all the emotions I felt about Steve came bubbling to the surface. I lost it emotionally. I began to weep uncontrollably, and I couldn't stop.

As the end credits rolled I tried to control my feelings but to no avail. The house lights went on, and I was still crying. Tears flooded down my face in a way they never had before. Embarrassed beyond words, I tried to hide my face as we left the crowded theater. Annalisa drove me back to my home. I cried almost all the way there. I was able to say "I'm sorry" to her a few times, but nothing more. I would struggle to regain my composure, and I would for a few short minutes at a time, but then it would start again. At home, alone, all was quiet as I laid in bed and cried myself to sleep. The next morning I realized that I had finally passed through the grieving period for my friend. I would shed no more tears. Not for the time being anyway. From now on when I thought or spoke of Steve it would always be with a smile on my face, and usually there would be the sound of laughter from the people who would listen to my stories of my dear friend.

www.ingramcontent.com/pod-product-compliance
Ingram Content Group UK Ltd.
Pitfield, Milton Keynes, MK11 3LW, UK
UKHW020245240426
12048UKWH00026B/1627